Problem-Based Learning

Second Edition

For all teachers who challenge their students to ask good questions and search for answers.

Second Edition

Problem-Based Learning

An **Inquiry** Approach

John Barell

CORWIN PRESS
A SAGE Publications Company
Thousand Oaks, CA 91320

For information:

Corwin Press
A Sage Publications Company
2455 Teller Road
Thousand Oaks, California 91320
www.corwinpress.com

Sage Publications Ltd.
1 Oliver's Yard
55 City Road
London EC1Y 1SP
United Kingdom

Sage Publications India Pvt. Ltd.
B-42, Panchsheel Enclave
Post Box 4109
New Delhi 110 017 India

Printed in the United States of America

Library of Congress Cataloging-in-Publication Data

Barell, John.
Problem-based learning: an inquiry approach / John Barell.—2nd ed.
     p. cm.
Title of 1st ed.: PBL.
Includes bibliographical references and index.
ISBN 1-4129-5003-1 or 978-1-4129-5003-9 (cloth)
ISBN 1-4129-5004-X or 978-1-4129-5004-6 (pbk.)
    1. Problem-based learning—United States. I. Barell, John. PBL. II. Title.
LB1027.42.B37 2007
371.39—dc22

                                                                2006023256

This book is printed on acid-free paper.

06   07   08   09   10   10   9   8   7   6   5   4   3   2   1

Acquisitions Editor:	Hudson Perigo
Editorial Assistant:	Jordan Barbakow
Production Editor:	Catherine M. Chilton
Copy Editor:	Kristin Bergstad
Typesetter:	C&M Digitals (P) Ltd.
Proofreader:	Doris Hus
Indexer:	Maria Sosnowski
Cover Designer:	Monique Hahn
Graphic Designer:	Lisa Miller

Contents

Acknowledgments

Thanks so much to the entire Corwin staff, especially Jean Ward, for your very careful, expert attention to this second edition. I appreciate your commitment to the principles of problem-based learning, an inquiry approach.

About the Author

John Barell is Professor Emeritus of Curriculum and Teaching at Montclair State University, Montclair, NJ, and former public school teacher in New York City. For the past several years he has been a consultant for inquiry-based instruction and creation of science/social studies networks at the American Museum of Natural History in New York City. For most of his educational career he has worked with schools nationally to foster inquiry, problem-based learning, critical thinking, and reflection.

He is the author of several books, including *Teaching for Thoughtfulness: Strategies to Enhance Intellectual Development* (1995, 2nd ed.) and *Developing More Curious Minds* (2003).

John Barell lives in New York City and can be reached at jbarell@nyc.rr.com.

Introduction

People ask me why I keep going back to Antarctica again and again. Well, I like it there. I like the endless reaches of wind-rippled snow, the stark peaks, the awesome glaciers. . . . Most of all, I guess, I like the challenge of it, for Antarctica still plays for keeps. And I believe, as the scientists do, that the things we can learn there will have a profound effect upon the lives of us all.

—Rear Admiral Richard E. Byrd

TRANSFORMATIONAL EXPERIENCE

Once there was a seventh grader who read a book that was full of adventures, daring exploits, dangerous journeys, and rewarding conquests. The book, *Alone* (1938) by Admiral Richard E. Byrd, describes a continent full of mystery. Increasingly, tourists are discovering the majesty of Antarctica, a mass of land covered by ice (in some places three miles thick), where temperatures dive down to −120 degrees Fahrenheit and winds screech at hurricane force. It is not very hospitable, but Antarctica is unspeakably beautiful.

For many reasons the young seventh grader was captivated by stories from the heroic age of exploration (about Amundsen, Scott, Shackleton, Byrd) and he wanted to know more. His continual questioning about this complex, earthly puzzle led to a wide variety of inquiry approaches: reading books, drawing charts, writing letters, building models, keeping a journal, conducting in-person interviews with explorers, visiting ships that sailed to Antarctica, setting goals to reach there, designing strategies to reach those goals, eventually reaching the continent, and setting out on explorations of his own.

These are just some of the inquiry strategies he used, mainly on his own as the result of reading that book, which was suggested by his grandmother. He continued to gather and reflect on new discoveries made by scientists from all over the world and to entertain new, more challenging questions.

This ongoing learning situation is what Perkins (personal communication, July 1992) has called a transformational experience, one that changes your life. And it certainly did that for this seventh grade boy, who is the author of this book.

Exploring Antarctica is my model of being an inquisitive person, setting off on fascinating explorations and making amazing discoveries. It is a metaphor for a life of inner adventure and discovery as an educator.

JOURNEY OF THOUGHT

This book is titled *Problem Based Learning: An Inquiry Approach* because developing questions about complex, intriguing, and sometimes mysterious experiences or phenomena seems to be a very natural occurrence. When people encounter strange happenings or difficult concepts and ideas, they naturally formulate questions such as, "What is going on? Why is this happening? What does this mean? What will happen in the future?" If they decide to answer these questions, they embark on a journey of thought that may take a few minutes, hours, or years. This book helps teachers create environments wherein they and their students can work with complex, intriguing situations that foster inquiry, research, and the drawing of reasonable conclusions.

STOP AND THINK

At various points in this text, there are places for you, the reader, to stop and reflect on a question. This is an opportunity to generate your own ideas and then compare them with those of others. The purpose of the Stop and Think sections is to elicit a wide variety of ideas and get teachers thinking about how to use inquiry for problem-based learning (PBL).

There is also a What's My Thinking Now? page at the end of each chapter. This page offers readers an opportunity to reflect on the chapter and jot down any comments or questions they may have—ones they may want to research later.

TRANSFORMATIONAL ELEMENTS

Not all school-based learning experiences can be called transformational; however, the premise of this book is that with students, teachers can design learning opportunities that build on the inquiry process. Inquiry, posing questions, is important for several reasons:

- Inquiry is a natural process, one people engage in from the time they begin to experiment with language
- Thinking begins with problematic situations, ones characterized by doubt, perplexity, and uncertainty
- Thinking through such dilemmas often leads to meaningful discoveries and then more and more questions
- The process is transferable from any one situation to another, across all cultures and ages

Stop and Think

 Identify a transformational experience of your own, one that may have begun with a complex situation that invited problem solving or long-range investigation.

What were the essential elements within this experience, elements that might be found in other people's experiences, ones that might be transferable to other experiences for adults and youngsters?

Here are some essential elements found in others' experiences:

- Identifying an intriguing phenomenon
- Making choices
- Generating lots of questions
- Being self-directed
- Searching for answers in many different places with a wide variety of people
- Learning teamwork
- Learning in new and exciting ways
- Setting goals and achieving them
- Sharing information with others
- Reflecting on the process continually

PBL AS AN INQUIRY PROCESS

This book uses the inquiry process to introduce PBL. It explains how to create an invitational environment, then walks the reader through three phases of PBL. It begins with the teacher-directed approach in which the teacher presents students with a problem to solve. The text then moves to a teacher-student shared inquiry in which students begin to direct some of their own learning. The final approach discussed is student-directed inquiry in which students become more self-directed learners. All three of these phases include sample units for the reader to use as models. Also included is an explanation of how to use PBL in the multidisciplinary classroom. The text ends with a discussion of how to assess this inquiry-based approach to learning and, possibly more important, how to transfer the learning to life outside of the classroom.

PART 1

Preparation

CHAPTER 1

An Inquiry Process

WORKING DEFINITION OF PBL

PBL (problem-based learning) can be defined as an inquiry process that resolves questions, curiosities, doubts, and uncertainties about complex phenomena in life. A problem is any doubt, difficulty, or uncertainty that invites or needs some kind of resolution. Student inquiry is very much an integral part of PBL and problem resolution.

Thus, in this book, PBL is presented as a way of challenging students to become deeply involved in a quest for knowledge—a search for answers to their own questions, not just answers to questions posed by a textbook or a teacher. Identifying problematic situations within the curriculum, posing questions, researching, and reporting depend on and foster a community of inquiry. In such a community, participants feel free to pose tough questions, learn from and build upon each other's questions, are open to different points of view, listen to and respect each other's ideas, and can work collaboratively toward reasonable conclusions.

IMPORTANCE OF PBL

Imagine life as problem-free. Wouldn't that be wonderful!

Or, would it?

In any case, life does not come problem-free because that is the nature of our life here on earth, full of challenging opportunities to learn, grow, reflect, and enjoy. This may be the most obvious reason why problem-based learning is important for us to consider—PBL engages students in life as we know it, full of fascinating problematic situations worth thinking about, investigating, and resolving.

Stop and Think

Why do you think PBL is so important in today's educational settings?

The following are some research-based reasons for the importance of PBL:

- Processing information at higher levels, such as with problem solving, critical thinking, inquiry strategies, and reflection on practice, leads to deeper understanding (Perkins, 1992), self-direction (McCombs, 1991), and enhanced retention and transferability of information and concepts (Bransford, Brown, & Cocking, 2000; Marzano, 2003; Marzano, Pickering, & Pollock, 2001; Mayer, 1989)

- Authentic pedagogy—involving knowledge construction, disciplined inquiry, and connections beyond school—results in higher student achievement, regardless of race, class, gender, or SES (Newmann & Associates, 1996).

- Teaching for understanding requires complex intellectual processes such as those involved in PBL—the need to analyze and process information and draw reasonable conclusions (Barell, 1995, 2003; Perkins, 1992). "Learning with understanding is more likely to promote transfer than simply memorizing information from a text or a lecture" (Bransford et al., 2000, p. 236).

- Several intellectual and pedagogical processes normally involved in PBL—including comparing/contrasting, summarizing, nonlinguistic representations, cooperative learning, generating and testing hypotheses, and questioning—have been shown to positively affect student achievement (Marzano et al., 2001).

- High levels of intellectual challenge and social interaction can be very motivating for many students (informal observations).

- PBL is inquiry- and choice-driven. These will be motivational elements for most students, opportunities to think and make choices with peers.

- "Expertise requires well-organized knowledge of concepts, principles, and procedures of inquiry," the latter playing a significant role in all forms of PBL (Bransford et al., 2000).

- "Learning requires multiple exposure to and complex interactions with knowledge." During a PBL unit students engage knowledge, skills and attitudes in many and varied contexts, rather than sitting and listening to information (Marzano, 2003).

- Informal observation indicates that some students with learning difficulties (or students who find the traditional classroom routines constraining) are challenged toward more lively and alternative engagements with and responses to content when they have opportunities to make some decisions about what and how to learn on their own.

- Inquiry-as-a-thread can be a way of integrating all instructional and curricular processes (as can cooperative learning and the use of fundamental concepts).

- The world of work requires the very intellectual skills fostered by PBL: problem solving, decision making, creative thinking, visualizing, critical reasoning, and knowing how to learn (SCANS, 1991).

- In controlled experiments, students in PBL classes showed a significant increase in the use of problem-solving strategies and these students gained as much, sometimes more, factual content than students in more traditional classrooms (Stepien, Gallagher, & Workman, 1992).

- Intriguing research from the medical community suggests PBL directly and positively affects the transfer and integration of concepts into clinical problems (Norman, 1992); and in certain PBL classrooms, one study found an increased use of hypothesis-driven reasoning and greater coherence in students' explanations (Hmelo, 1994).

Stop and Think

 Can you think of other reasons for trying PBL? How do the above research findings highlight what you see occurring in classrooms today?

In focusing upon complex, authentic problematic situations PBL affords us an opportunity to examine such experiences from multiple perspectives. Thus, PBL can be more interdisciplinary than pursuing questions within only one subject area.

Perhaps these findings also lead us to examine our classrooms for the extent of reasoning (Goodlad, 1984) and/or the opportunities for transfer of ideas to novel or real-life situations (Bransford et al., 2000; Mayer, 1989). Such research can provide reasons for observing what does occur in classrooms in terms of students' not only receiving information but also, and more importantly, processing (e.g., analyzing) and applying it. What PBL does in all its forms is to provide students with challenges—to encounter a complex situation, to engage in analysis, information gathering, critical thinking about findings and drawing reasonable conclusions.

Another reason for fostering PBL with an inquiry approach is what state and subject matter standards demand. We'll refer to this more in subsequent chapters, but let me cite a goal from the New York State Regents, the group responsible for New York state's educational policy:

Goal 2: Each student will be able to apply methods of inquiry and knowledge learned through all major disciplines and use the methods and knowledge in interdisciplinary applications.

Finally, it goes without saying that at the commencement of the twenty-first century, the problems we face in foreign and domestic affairs, the effects of globalization, and the changes in nature, that we must educate students to be able to identify important problems, ask probing questions, and conduct rigorous investigations aimed at finding answers and solutions. If we fail to educate for inquiry, problem solving, critical/creative thinking, and reflection, our ways of life will surely be in peril. It is our duty as citizens of this republic to become well-informed inquirers and seekers after reasonable solutions to the problems that affect our quality of life here and around the globe.

ELEMENTS OF PBL

Within any PBL unit you are likely to encounter the following elements:

Problem Statement—often in scenario form: "You are a paleontologist (or city planner) responsible for . . ."

Various roles to be assumed by students

Opportunities to analyze situation, raise questions

Investigations—often within collaborative groups—to search for answers

Critical analysis of findings and drawing of reasonable conclusions

Findings to share, presentations often in front of peers or interested/informed audiences

Various kinds of assessments—informal and formal, authentic, by students and teachers

These elements will, of course, vary by students' ages and abilities, but each PBL has as its core a problematic situation to be addressed.

PBL STRATEGIES

PBL crosses a broad spectrum of instructional patterns, from total teacher control to more emphasis on self-directed student inquiry. Patterns of power and control over decision making are affected by what Fullan (1993) calls "reculturing" the school. That is, if teachers alter patterns of who makes what kinds of instructional decisions, when and how within the classroom, teachers affect the deep structure of the school. PBL can be defined as change in curriculum that can significantly affect the culture of the entire school.

The two major strategies to foster problem posing and inquiry are derived from prereading strategies and good scientific observation processes. The first is KWHLAQ:

K What do we think we already **Know** about the subject?

W What do we **Want/Need** to find out about it?

H **How** and where will we search for answers? How will we organize our investigations (e.g., Time, Access to Resources, and Reporting)?

L What do we expect to **Learn**? What have we **Learned**?

A How will we **Apply** what we have learned to other subjects? To our personal lives? To our next projects?

Q What new **Questions** do we have following our inquiry?

This strategy derives from the K-W-L (Olge, 1986), a prereading strategy designed to engage students in thinking about prior knowledge and the purposes for reading. An earlier version of the KWHLAQ (Barell, 1995) sought to expand this limited application to longer-term curricular units of instruction.

The second major strategy is O-T-Q:

O **Observe** objectively

T **Think** reflectively

Q **Question** frequently

O-T-Q derives from research (Barell, 1992) on inquiry with third graders. When asked to generate questions about recent visits to museums, Disney World, or historical sites, most students had real difficulties forming questions. What helped was drawn from what scientists do: First observe and gather information, then analyze and relate the information to what they know, and finally generate questions.

Figure 1.1 is a display of these strategies within the spectrum of teacher control. The KWHLAQ and O-T-Q are squarely in between total teacher power over decisions and student-controlled decision making. This placement is for illustration purposes only. Obviously, teachers can use either strategy at either end of the spectrum and often do.

Figure 1.1   Problem-Based Learning Spectrum of Strategies

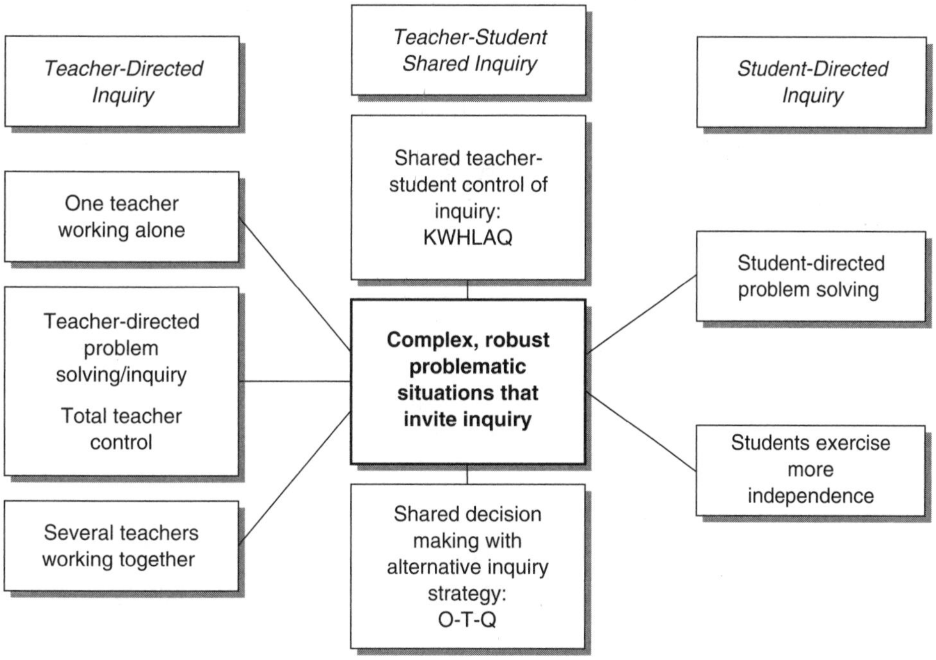

EXAMPLES OF PBL EXPERIENCES

Several teachers already challenge their students with various kinds of PBL experiences, most of which involve inquiry of some sort. Here is a brief description of some of their inquiry projects:

- Kindergartners with some learning difficulties posing questions to figure out what the water cycle is and determining how to explain it to an NBC executive searching for a "weather person." (Newark, NJ)
- Third graders posing questions about why sun flares "fall out into space," why school buses are painted yellow, how people dressed thousands of years ago, and why there are no women presidents (yet!)? (Peg Murray, Bradford Elementary School, Upper Montclair, NJ)
- Fifth graders investigating what life was like during World War II from survivors in the local community (Robin Cayce, Chattanooga, TN)
- Middle school students with learning difficulties want to figure out what law enforcement, education, and emergency services are needed for a new business relocating to your town (Ashland, WI)
- High school students in Spanish class have to figure out how to welcome the growing population of immigrants to their home town (St. Croix Falls, WI)
- Tenth-grade biology students hypothesizing about the extent of bacteria within the school, conducting research, analyzing findings, and reporting (Vin Frick, Dumont High School, Dumont, NJ)
- Twelfth graders in political science class respond to their own question, "If I want to become president of the United States, how do I go about getting elected?" Their research consists of selecting candidates, holding caucuses, and running for election (Ed Bertolini, Jefferson Township High School, Oakridge, NJ)
- Twelfth-grade Chemistry students must determine whether or not to approve the construction of a nuclear power plant for their community (LoriAnn Davide, James Caldwell High School, Caldwell, NJ)

Most of these experiences can fit within one or more of the elements of the PBL Spectrum of Strategies (see Figure 1.1). Some reflect different phases of the spectrum of control (the horizontal axis), from complete teacher control on the left to more student self-directed learning on the right.

How often PBL can be used involves such considerations as time, resources, ability and maturity of students, school culture and climate for inquiry and research, basic beliefs in the nature of teaching and learning, and the amount of commitment to these principles.

Each reflects the presence of a significant problematic situation worth investigating. What do you notice about each of these problematic situations? What characteristics do they have in common? Here are some I'm sure you have noticed:

Complex: They have no easy, obvious answers found within a book and invite interdisciplinary investigations from multiple perspectives.

Fascinating: They are fun to investigate, often with teams of students.

Meaningful: They relate to our major curricular objectives as well as to our own lives.

Authentic: They often come from life as we know it.

Problem-based learning allows us an opportunity to conduct investigations that are also

Inquiry- and choice-driven, each requiring decisions about what is important, what we need to know, and how we will find answers

Team/group organized, allowing for collaboration at all stages

Intellectually challenging, requiring problem solving and critical analysis in order to figure out answers/solutions

Conclusive, each able to lead us to making judgments based on well-researched evidence

When curriculum is arranged and focused upon such intriguing problematic situations, we will notice something different happening—students of very different abilities and interests will become involved in ways we haven't observed before. Students with learning difficulties and those with previously low achievement records might become far more interested and involved because we are presenting them with opportunities to make choices, take more ownership of their own learning, and to express themselves in different fashions.

On the other hand, we may also find that our previously high achievers have some difficulty with this format because it does not involve "Guess what's on the teacher's mind and what's going to be on the test." PBL presents them with challenges quite different from memorizing content presented by the teacher. It is far more challenging and breaks routines and boundaries previously held sacred within the classroom.

Jack Welch, previously CEO of General Electric, transformed this company with a concept called "boundaryless," meaning he broke down traditional lines of authority among leaders, managers, and employees in order to get the best minds working on complex problems. In a way, PBL represents this kind of "boundarylessness" in our classrooms (Welch, 2001, p. 186).

PBL of this nature requires that we establish a classroom environment that welcomes questioning and different points of view and that thrives on collaboration among all participants.

What's My Thinking Now

Reflection

Comments

Questions

CHAPTER 2

Designing the Invitational Environment

HOW ENVIRONMENT AFFECTS INQUIRY

During a reflective session on a long-range inquiry project I asked several teachers what they had learned about inquiry. Here are some of their comments:

- Very involving
- Creates sense of student ownership and empowerment
- Not always easy to come up with good questions
- Risky to share your ignorance
- Requires good group work: sharing control, listening, and learning from each other
- Must have sufficient background knowledge to ask any questions at all
- Results in longer-term learning than listening to lectures
- Requires that we feel comfortable with taking risks

All of these statements are valid, but it is the last one—feeling comfortable taking risks—that is the focus here. What the teacher seemed to be referring to was that people will not jump into a complex situation to ask questions or challenge another point of view unless they feel secure about what is known and not known, feel the assurance that questions will be received well, and feel that everyone is in this together. In essence, it's difficult for a teacher to carry out problem-based learning (PBL) without first considering the classroom environment.

Consequently, this chapter deals with establishing a classroom environment where trust, open communication, and willingness to take risks without fear of negative consequences prevail. This is an environment that invites students to participate in several of the most significant adventures of their lives—asking questions, searching for answers, creating meaningful relationships, and reflecting on their journey. Educators want, as one teacher so aptly

put it, to establish a partnership for learning. Such a partnership is one of the essential elements within the community of inquiry.

Stop and Think

 Reflect on those core values, beliefs, behaviors, and attitudes you would like to foster and develop among all of your students during the course of a year—behaviors that would contribute to creating a community of inquiry. Here is a list of behaviors you might select from:

openness to mystery, alternative points of view	self-respect	accuracy
	curiosity	good listening
	empathy	confidence
tolerance	sense of humor	considers others' feelings, ideas
independence, self-direction	honesty	
	efficiency	being objective
respect for others and their ideas	persistence	fairness
	deliberateness	points of view
cooperation	fun	

What four intended outcome behaviors are the most important to you? Which one of those four behaviors do you think is the most fundamental, the one you would foster and develop if you could choose only one to become integrated throughout the entire curriculum and within the school as a whole?

Imagine your school graduating students who demonstrate each of your core behaviors and values. How would life be different—for them, for you? How can you foster any one of these behaviors—by modeling, by teaching them directly?

REDESIGNING CLASSROOMS

One seventh- and eighth-grade science teacher, on opening day, gave his students a list of what they would learn. That year, the first item was not science ideas (that was number ten!). Respect for each others' ideas was first. Given the age group and the necessity to work collaboratively in science, this seems appropriate.

Others have focused on fostering student curiosity and willingness to follow through on their own questions. These behaviors become very important in the community that fosters the basis of PBL.

Regardless of which behaviors we select to focus on, there are certain elements we need to develop throughout the teaching year to establish an environment of inquiry. These elements include the following:

Teacher modeling: thinking aloud through problematic situations

Questioning: teacher and student questions

Quality responding: how teachers respond to statements/questions/ expressions of feelings does more to foster open communications than their questions

Peer interacting: creating a setting for responding positively and questioning each other

Developing group inquiry skills: researching, critically thinking about information (e.g., determining bias, using evidence to draw reasonable conclusions, avoiding plagiarism) listening, focusing on the topic, building on each others' ideas, developing consensus, and so forth

Using Reflective Journals: questioning across the curriculum

Now comes the fun part: using these elements to redesign classrooms and schools to foster these kinds of behaviors. If teachers want students to develop and live these behaviors, they need to start off the educational year with a conducive environment.

FIRST WEEK'S EXPERIENCES

A teacher recently asked the following question during a workshop on Developing More Curious Minds: "Would it be reasonable to take the first week (or two) of school to establish the community of inquiry, to get students comfortable with confronting strange, complex problems, learning how to ask good questions, how to cooperate and listen to each other and to think critically about information they gather in searching for answers?"

What do you think? Is this an important step to take if we want to foster the behaviors identified above and we're going to work with problem-based learning? See Figure 2.1.

My colleague during this workshop, Shehla Ghouse, and I responded with a resounding, "Yes!"

Here are several strategies we should employ from the beginning of school in September to create this community of inquiry.

TEACHER MODELING

A model is someone or something that represents the kinds of behaviors, relationships, or parts people hold up to themselves and others as exemplary. There are fashion models, model cars and airplanes, and models of economic conditions. Research (Bandura, 1986) suggests that modeling good behaviors, such as problem solving, is a good way for students to learn them. Teacher modeling helps to foster the invitational environment because when teachers relate their own experiences, they can communicate several messages:

- Teachers confront problems in and out of school daily
- Sometimes teachers solve problems well
- Other times teachers are not as successful

OPENING WEEK EXPERIENCES

Teacher Modeling

Recent experiences of questioning nature, events, human relations, authorities

O-T-Q

Students observing, thinking/relating to prior knowledge, and generating questions about artifacts, experiences, media and the like

Arranging the Physical Setting

Ensure that the physical setting of the room is conducive to inquiry and responding to each other

Teachable Moments in Class

Classroom problematic situations that call for questions and investigations

Figure 2.1

DESIGN YOUR OWN OPENING WEEK LEARNING EXPERIENCES TO FOSTER DESIRED BEHAVIORS

Desired Behaviors

Teacher Modeling of Inquisitiveness

Observe, Think, and Question

Questioning of Content Factoids/Problematic Situations

Introduction of Inquiry Journals

Use of Frameworks (see Figure 2.3) to Analyze Our Questions

Developing Good Listening/Responding/Cooperative Behaviors and Attitudes

Initiating Critical Analysis of Information for Reliability of Sources, Evidence, Assumptions, Definitions, and Balance

When teachers share both successful and not so successful experiences with students, they let students know that they are not perfect. Teachers do not have all the answers. Teachers are, in other words, vulnerable. This helps establish the climate of partnership: Teachers and students are in this together.

Teachers need to act as models for their students, showing students how they deal with problematic situations. Teachers need to model the kinds of behaviors and dispositions (such as curiosity, persistence, open-mindedness) they want their students to learn. For example, a teacher might tell students about confronting the problem of having to purchase a new computer. The teacher might share these kinds of questions:

- What's the nature of the problem I have with the old computer?
- What do I want/need to do? What's my plan?
- What information do I need? What questions should I ask myself before buying something impulsively?
- How and where will I find answers and what criteria will I use to make a decision?
- How will I know if I have succeeded?

The teacher could tell students about all the resources he or she considered: people, the Internet, stores, magazines, and so forth. The teacher could tell students about his or her decision-making process and how well it worked or is working.

Stop and Think

 What kinds of problems or issues do you encounter daily? Which can you share with students? What kinds of questions do you often or seldom ask? Why? Within which kinds of situations should you ask certain kinds of questions?

TEACHERS' KEEPING AN INQUIRY JOURNAL

One of the best ways to begin a process of modeling our problem-solving and questioning processes is for each of us to commence keeping a journal within which we write down the kinds of problems we encounter daily, how we approach them, the kinds of questions we ask, how we work through them, and our assessment of the achieved results.

Using this form of journal will give us necessary experience in observing, reflecting upon, and evaluating our own thinking.

As we spend time observing, reflecting upon, and evaluating our own thinking, we gain confidence in the kinds of intellectual processes we engage in and those we seem to overlook.

For example, when encountering a problem, do we sometimes rush to find a solution without stepping back, saying "Wait. What is the real problem here? Do I need to solve it? If so, what are my alternatives? What questions do I need to ask? Who can help me?"

When we've achieved a level of confidence reflecting on our own thinking, we can begin sharing some of our experiences with students in the classroom. You will be able to share not only the problems and the processes you followed, but also, and perhaps more important, you will be able to share with them what you are learning about your own problem-solving and inquiry processes. The latter might be the most important kind of modeling for them to witness.

OBSERVE, THINK, AND QUESTION (O-T-Q)

An important way to foster inquiry on a regular basis is to share some complex, puzzling, and perplexing situation, picture, or experience with students on a regular basis.

I've used a picture of a fossil-like critter found in a rock quarry in China. This pictures shows what appears to be a four-limbed, large-headed creature, with seemingly sharp teeth, a pointed snout, thick neck, long tail, and very thin amber colored lines ("filaments," the paleontologists called them) emanating from head, neck, and torso areas that some observers immediately conclude are "fur" or "feathers" (Norell, 2001).

I tell students that they are to assume the role of paleontologists on an expedition, charged with analyzing this critter and developing a line of inquiry to determine its nature, history, and similarities to other creatures of the geological period. This puts them into problem-based learning mode immediately.

Then we divide the class into small groups and ask each to appoint an observer to keep track of observations, reflections on prior knowledge ("It looks like a bird, a fossil, a dinosaur. . . ."), and questions they have.

After several minutes we elicit their findings and spend more time examining the kinds of questions they have posed. I ask, "What do you notice about your questions? What do they have in common?" (Sometimes even adults ask questions that seem as if they can be answered "Yes" or "No" or with one-word responses.

Then what do we do?

We examine an array or framework of different kinds of questions with which to compare our own so that, over time, we can improve upon the kinds of questions we pose (see Figure 2.3).

What pictures, artifacts, stories, and experiences might you use at the beginning of school to foster students' abilities to observe closely, relate to prior knowledge, and generate a host of good questions? Teachers have used quilts, poetry, pictures of natural phenomena, a short visit to a nearby pond or park, and newspaper articles and stories.

DIFFERENT KINDS OF QUESTIONS AND THEIR INTELLECTUAL DEMANDS

One of the best tools for teachers and their students is a questioning framework that also serves as a model for how the mind functions during productive

Figure 2.3 Three-Story Intellect

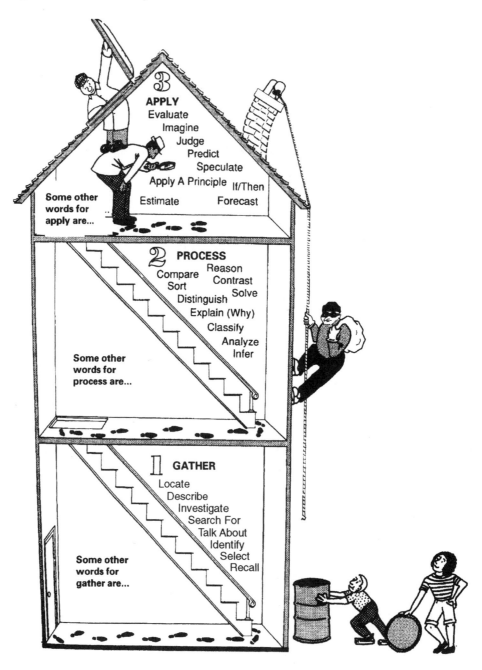

SOURCE: From *Problem-Based Learning & Other Curriculum Models for the Multiple Intelligences Classroom,* by Robin Fogarty, 1997.

thought. Such a model is the Three-Story Intellect (see Figure 2.3). This model provides teachers with a way of thinking about how students learn for deep understanding. Students need to gather information through a variety of means. They need to process and apply it to develop a deep understanding and sense of ownership of the knowledge or skill. So much of classroom discourse still seems to focus on only one of the levels of the three-story intellect model.

As you can see, there are three levels of verbs that represent the intellectual demands of students. A teacher can model each level of questioning in the following fashion:

Level I: What is this object?

Level II: With what would you compare it?

Level III: Is this a good specimen of a creature that lived a long time ago? Why do you think so?

Each question requires of the respondents a different level of intellectual challenge.

Then we can return to our Observe, Think, and Question (O-T-Q) list of students' questions and ask students to compare their questions with Levels I, II, and III. What kinds did they ask?

Next, we can ask them to experiment with asking questions they might not have asked, for example:

Level I: What are this critter's prominent features/characteristics?

Level II: To what other Triassic period animals could we compare this critter? Do you think this critter was capable of flight? Could it be a transition between dinosaurs and birds? Explain your reasoning.

Level III: Imagine this critter's being alive today. In what kind of environment would it survive? Who would be its natural predators?

If we engage in this kind of O-T-Q experience weekly (prior to engaging in a fully developed PBL unit described later), students will become very good at asking a wide range of questions.

And, when students keep a problem-solving/Inquiry Journal in which they weekly record their original and revised questions, they can periodically reflect on their growth in becoming good questioners, and we will have informal assessment information.

Stop and Think

 Select a topic from one of your units of study and find a problematic situation, image, or statement within it. Present this to students to engage in an Observe, Think, and Question experience, thereby enhancing their observational and questioning skills.

Another aspect of the three-story intellect model is that it helps teachers understand the crucial roles of all three levels. Namely, students need information with which to think (Level I). Then students need to process it to achieve a degree of understanding (Level II) and finally to use it in some content (Level III).

These three levels fit Perkins's (1992) identification of education's three primary goals: retain, understand, and apply information.

Carla Coelho-Chu (Pleasantdale School, West Orange, NJ) used the three-story intellect model when creating questions for her second-grade class. The following are questions she used and modeled for a unit on rocks:

Questions	Intellectual Demands
How do rocks form?	Recall/problem solving*
How are rocks different?	Compare/contrast/draw conclusions
What causes rocks to change?	Recall/problem solving
How do rocks form mountains?	Recall/problem solving
Are rocks important? Why?	Evaluate

* This question and others like it might involve students in reading and remembering a text that describes the three different kinds of rocks (sedimentary, igneous, and metamorphic) and how they form. But students might also have to look at an unfamiliar specimen and figure out how it came to be.

Carla chose questions that challenged students' thinking beyond finding simple answers in a book, from a person, or on the Internet.

FASCINATING FACTOIDS TO STIMULATE INQUIRY

It may also be interesting for teachers to consider a factoid, or an isolated fact, that might become more meaningful if considered at some length. The following factoid could generate several questions:

Nine hundred million years ago Earth's day was eighteen hours and ten minutes long (Source: *The New York Times*, Science Section, July 9, 1996). If we present this to students who have requisite background knowledge, we might omit the figures "18 hours and 10 minutes," then challenge students to ask good questions ("What do we know? Need to find out?"), analyze the problem, come to a conclusion, and explain their reasoning.

Then we can ask them what questions we need to ask in order to understand the scientific conclusion. For example:

How do we know?

Why was it different then?

How does this help us understand the forces operating on Earth, on the Moon, and within the solar system? How does our knowledge of planetary rotation, revolution, and gravity help us understand the situation?

What will it be 100 million years from now? 900 million years from now? How do we know?

Intellectual Demands

Determining sources/testing the reliability/validity of information and sources

Determining causal factors

Analyzing/comparing/contrasting/drawing conclusions

Understanding causal factors/prediction

Activities like this one can be used to help students delve more deeply into statements of fact. We tend to take them at face value without, for example, asking critical questions such as, "Who said so? Can we believe them? How do we know? How is this important now? In the future?" One significant aspect of PBL is knowing what kinds of critical thinking questions we need to ask in order to understand a situation or statement.

TEACHERS' QUALITY RESPONDING

Sigel (personal communication, May 1990) of Educational Testing Service in Princeton, New Jersey, once suggested that how a teacher responds to students' comments and questions may be more important than the questions the teacher asks. After a career of investigating how to develop students' intellectual abilities, Sigel concluded that the teacher's tone of voice, the teacher's way of attending to the students, and the teacher's interest in the students' ideas could communicate a great deal that would contribute to creating the invitational environment.

If the question is "What metaphors can you imagine that compare the relationship of England and the thirteen colonies before the Revolutionary War?" one student response could be, "It's like a kid breaking away from home." One good teacher response would be, "How interesting! Help me understand how you arrived at that comparison." Another teacher response, less likely to foster in-depth reflection would be, "That's crazy! I've never heard of anything as far-out in my life!"

Stop and Think

 How would you respond to this student?

Most responses can be classified under these categories:

Empathize with feelings: "I feel the same way at times. Can you share with us what brought about these feelings?"

Elicit good reasons: "Interesting! How do you see these two as similar?"

Elaborate upon an idea: "Please tell me more about your thinking/your ideas."

Provide more specific information or examples: "Can you give us more details about this comparison? Can you give us some examples?"

Clarify: "It isn't quite clear to me how parental imposition of house rules, like 'Be home at 12 o'clock,' is similar to what England did. Can you help me understand?"

Relate to others' comments: "How do your ideas relate to Jennifer's?"

Build upon others' ideas: "Can you add to what Jennifer has said?"

Reflect metacognitively: "I wonder how you thought of that comparison. Could you tell us please?"

The aim is to communicate genuine interest in knowing more about the student's thoughts and feelings. By tone of voice, physical attitude toward the person (distance, leaning toward the student), and facial expressions, teachers communicate their concern and desire to know more about what the student said. One student once said about her teacher, "Just watch his eyebrows if you want to know what he thinks!"

GENERATING PEER INTERACTION AND DISCUSSION

In an article titled "Research on Questioning and Discussion," Dillon (1984) suggested there is a variety of verbal interaction in the classroom. At one end of the spectrum is what he refers to as the quiz show (i.e., guess what's on the teacher's mind). At the other end of the spectrum is genuine discussion in which different points of view are presented openly with the intention of arriving at a conclusion.

During a quiz show the student's role is to figure out the correct answer, very often known only to the teacher. Sometimes, teachers need to highlight the importance of a fact (e.g., Bill Gates was president of Microsoft) or define a principle (e.g., one of Newton's three laws of motion). There is nothing wrong with the quiz show, unless teachers rely on it as their only or primary strategy.

A good discussion, on the other hand, focuses on a complex question or issue. Participants attempt to reason toward their own and perhaps a general conclusion based on evidence while listening to a wide diversity of points of view. A question such as, "What will Bill Gates's company be doing in 40 or 100 years?" generates this kind of intense involvement where there are multiple responses that are possible and reasonable.

Thus, quiz shows and discussions have different roles to play in the classroom, with the latter being very important for creating the invitational environment.

Here are some suggestions for creating genuine discussions:

- Ensure that everyone knows the names of all classmates from the very beginning
- Encourage students to respond to each other's comments and not just to the teacher's (e.g., a third-grade teacher can tell students to address the previous speaker when responding: "David, I agree/disagree with your ideas, because. . . ." She learned this technique from Lipman's Philosophy for Children program [Lipman, Sharp, & Oscanyan, 1980].)
- Use good follow-up responses (e.g., "Nick, what do you think of Carriann's comment? Kelly, do you agree with Mike's thinking? Why or why not?")
- When a student asks a question, respond by asking other students for an answer (e.g., "Who has an answer to Jessica's question?" This is an attempt to get the whole class involved and to move away from the model of the coach throwing the ball out to each player and receiving it back from him or her. The intellectual ball should be thrown among the players as it is during a real game. In the classroom the students should be the players!)
- Ask students what the components of a good discussion are, post their ideas, and use them as guidelines; then ask, "How well are we doing in our discussions?"
- Use small groups to help students become less shy about participating, and sit in on these discussions while they are being held
- Create a modeling situation with students, perhaps from another class or grade, to show your students what a good discussion can look like (e.g., a first-grade teacher can ask some fourth graders to present a negative model, then her children can create their own guidelines for good discussions)
- Model good listening and eye contact, and attend to everyone's comments
- Write in Reflective Journals and answer questions such as, "How well do you think our discussion went today? How can we improve on our performance?"

Stop and Think

 How can you use these strategies to generate genuine discussions with your students? What else can you do to encourage genuine discussions with your students?

STUDENTS' REFLECTIVE JOURNALS

Plato, through the voice of Socrates, once observed that, "The unexamined life is not worth living" (Cooper, 1977, p. 38). Dewey (1963) noted that, "Thinking is the accurate and deliberate instituting of connections between what is done and its consequences" (p. 151). For Dewey, it is reflection on activities that make them meaningful experiences. One way to organize these reflections is by writing about them after they have occurred with an attempt to make the connections Dewey mentioned.

Journals provide such opportunities, and the writing and subsequent sharing of reflections can contribute significantly to developing a community of inquiry.

Two journal formats might be helpful here. One, a formal entry, consists of responding to questions such as, "What was my problem to solve? How did I go about solving it? (Describe your thought processes, not the answer.) How would I evaluate my problem-solving processes? What might I do differently next time and why?" (Barell, 1995).

This formal entry is suitable for both mathematical/scientific problems with convergent answers and for more open-ended, complex situations such as those suggested with the Bill Gates questions.

More informal entries provide several writing options such as the stems in Figure 2.4.

Stop and Think

Select one of the informal journal stems and reflect on your experiences with PBL.

WHY THE ENVIRONMENT IS IMPORTANT TO PBL

Teachers modeling, asking different kinds of questions, engaging in Observe, Think, and Question exercises weekly with situations drawn from the subject, making quality responses, generating peer interaction and discussion, and using Reflective Journals are just some ways to foster an invitational environment. These strategies create an environment where students feel comfortable contributing, taking the risk of asking a "weird" question, or contradicting something the book or the teacher says. Without a solid foundation in good listening and having respect for everyone's ideas, teachers cannot establish the kinds of partnerships and communities of inquiry that are the foundation of any PBL strategy.

> The more safe/fair I make it to ask, make a mistake, take a chance, the better the kids feel about asking any of their questions and the more honest the inquiry. (Karen Kenny, Denver)

SENTENCE STEMS FOR REFLECTIVE JOURNALS

What seems important here is. . . .

What I would like to know more about is. . . .

I wonder. . . .

The important ideas/conclusions here are. . . .

This reminds me of. . . .

This relates or is connected to. . . .

What surprises/fascinates me is. . . .

What if. . . .

I feel. . . .

My tentative conclusions are. . . .

What I am learning about the subject, inquiry, and my own thinking processes. . . .

Figure 2.4

What's My Thinking Now

Reflection

Comments

Questions

CHAPTER 3

A Curricular Overview

MAJOR ELEMENTS OF THE CURRICULUM PROCESS

Teachers establish a community of inquiry over a long period of time while teaching all the important ideas, skills, and dispositions in the curriculum. What helps the discussion of problem-based learning (PBL) is to identify the foundational elements of curriculum on which PBL is based.

These elements include content, complex situations/problems worth investigating, objectives, teaching and learning strategies and, of course, assessments. All curricula, whether problem-based or more traditional, involve these elements in one way or another.

CONTENT

Content is composed of those concepts, ideas, principles, skills, and dispositions; it is important that students become engaged with content. Content also refers to the ways of knowing and the methods of inquiry within each subject. For example, within science we often learn "the scientific method," even though science does not always proceed in the strict fashion outlined in textbooks. In literature we have ways of figuring out meaning that can also be the focus of our units. In a landmark book by the same name, Parker (1970) identified "Process as Content," meaning we should learn the thinking processes associated with different subjects as well as learn key information, concepts, and principles. Among the most important processes to engage in, of course, is inquiry and, subsequently, conducting rigorous investigations guided by critical thinking.

In a unit on the Age of Exploration, teachers might say they want their students to think seriously about the concepts of change, leadership, and cultural exchange and domination and to become more accurate and persistent in historical analysis, identifying reliable (unbiased) sources, and drawing reasonable conclusions using varieties of supporting evidence. Here we have a mixture of concepts, ways of knowing, and dispositions.

Questions we can ask ourselves at this stage include, "What concepts are worth thinking about over a period of time?" Criteria for making this decision will include:

1. Which concepts are central to understanding the subject?

2. Which concepts are fascinating? Meaningful to students in a variety of ways?

3. Which concepts/principles/ways of knowing are robust—applicable across the board to other subjects and within our personal lives?

COMPLEX SITUATIONS/PROBLEMS WORTH INVESTIGATING

"You are a member of the town planning committee charged with welcoming new residents who do not speak English. You need to plan all the necessary elements of a welcome package, including visits to homes, school planning, employment briefings, and much more. How will you and your committee proceed?"

This is an example of a problematic situation that teachers might present to students to initiate learning about different cultures in a middle school classroom. As we shall see, such scenarios are very much a part of problem-based learning.

This complex, problematic situation is one that, according to Dewey (1933), will arouse thinking because it involves, doubt, difficulty, and uncertainty. It may be an empirical situation like the above and others, such as figuring out how to redesign an elementary school playground, figuring out how to get elected president, or determining the extent of bacterial contamination in a school. Or the problematic situation may be a more abstract, future-oriented experience such as trying to reason through the future of Microsoft or Google. This situation will start the inquiry, one that is complex and will grab students' interest and attention. This is the "problem" of PBL and it reflects Welch's "boundaryless" in its complexity and multifaceted nature.

This problem scenario should also contain elements of an authentic assessment of students' understanding. The more well-crafted the initiating scenario is, the better it provides bookends for the entire unit.

OBJECTIVES

Objectives are what teachers strive to accomplish. For the purpose of this book, this means asking the question, "What do I want my students to be able to do at unit's/year's end? What are my intended outcomes?" It is what students do that counts toward learning, not what the teacher does (Tyler, 1949). If the subject of the science lesson is photosynthesis, teachers need to think of what they want students to do with or about this concept. What will students be engaged in intellectually? Teachers might ask them to read from the text, or teachers might lecture or bring in demonstrations. But what are students going to do? Teachers need to decide if they are going to analyze, compare, create a model, draw conclusions, and so forth.

Perkins (1992) identified three major goals of education that help teachers think of what they want students to do:

Retain knowledge (e.g., Describe the conditions in Spain in 1492 when Columbus departed)

Understand it (e.g., Compare Columbus with a contemporary adventurer in terms of leadership ability and draw your own conclusions)

Apply/use it (e.g., Use your critical thinking skills to analyze a contemporary historical event to determine role of the leaders)

Our objectives *must* include Levels II and III of the Three-Story Intellect (see Figure 2.3) in order to ensure that students are thinking constructively about major concepts within the unit. These are the sine qua nons of challenging lessons and units. We must engage students in what Newmann and his associates (1996) call "cognitive work found in the adult world" (p. 24).

And, *even more important*, whatever we state as our objectives must be included in the assessment experiences we plan for the culmination of a unit. If the objectives call for decision making and model building, then our assessments must challenge students to make and analyze decisions as well as create and evaluate models.

CONTENT STANDARDS

Every state has rigorous curriculum content standards that guide teachers in selecting content for instruction in all subjects. Like most states, "New Jersey's standards were created to improve student achievement by clearly defining what all students should know and be able to do at the end of thirteen years of public education" ("Introduction," n.d.).

With respect to PBL, these curriculum content standards will identify the major concepts, principles, ideas, and skills all students need to understand and be able to apply in life. Specifically, New Jersey wants all students to master these critical thinking skills by Grade 8:

1. Communicate, analyze data, apply technology, and problem solve.

2. Describe how personal beliefs and attitudes affect decision making.

3. Identify and assess problems that interfere with attaining goals.

4. Recognize bias, vested interest, stereotyping, and the manipulation and misuse of information.

5. Practice goal setting and decision making in areas relative to life skills. ("Career Education and Consumer, Family, and Life Skills," 2005)

As Mark O'Shea (2005) has pointed out, standards may also include "an active-voice description of a student performance or product" (p. 51). This means that the standards can also help us identify what kinds of learning outcomes we ought to plan. For example, by Grade 8 in New Jersey, students should be able to do the following in a social studies class:

1. Analyze how events are related over time.

2. Use critical thinking skills to interpret events and to recognize bias, point of view, and context.

3. Assess the credibility of primary and secondary sources.

4. Analyze data in order to see persons and events in context.

5. Examine current issues, events, or themes and relate them to past events.

6. Formulate questions based on information needs.

7. Compare and contrast competing interpretations of current and historical events.

And by Grade 12 students in the same class should be able to:

1. Debate current issues and controversies involving the central ideas of the American constitutional system, including representative government (e.g., electoral college and the popular vote), civic virtue (e.g., increasing voter turnout through registrations and campaigns), checks and balances, and limits on governmental power.

2. Analyze, through current and historical examples and Supreme Court cases, the scope of governmental power and how the constitutional distribution of responsibilities seeks to prevent the abuse of that power.

3. Compare the American system of representative government with systems in other democracies such as the parliamentary systems in England and France. (based on New Jersey State Standards, 2004; see "Social Studies," 2006)

Notice the key words that guide our planning for assessments: *Analyze, assess, interpret, formulate, compare and contrast.*

These words closely resemble those at Levels II and III of the Three-Story Intellect (see Figure 2.3). Notice also the helpful suggestions for assessment by Grade 12 to debate current issues involving the American constitutional system.

State content standards, therefore, can be immensely helpful in preparing units of instruction. We must take them into account when formulating our problematic scenarios, objectives, assessments, and learning strategies. They can be productive guides in this regard and need not be considered straightjackets.

RESOURCES

Resources include everything from books, the Internet, and CD-ROMs to people, including teachers, adults in the community, and don't forget other students.

When thinking about students using the Internet we want also to follow the lead of Heidi Nyser of CES 11 in the Bronx, New York. For a third-grade integrated literature/science unit, while her students were investigating fascinating questions about the solar system, Heidi used "mini lessons" to teach students the difference between "fact and opinion, how to paraphrase and summarize, using context clues to determine the meaning of unknown words and how to avoid plagiarism." In effect, Heidi was teaching her third graders how to think critically about and responsibly use a wide variety of nonfiction resources (personal communication, June 2005)

Excellent Internet resources for science and literature are the following (as of May 2006):

http://www.amnh.org

http://www.refdesk.com

http://www.ask.com

http://www.google.com

Outstanding teacher resources replete with references to all kinds of pedagogical strategies and planning approaches in ALL subjects are

http://www.oops.bizland.com (Helen Teague of Abilene, TX)

http://school.discovery.com/schrockguide/index.html (Kathy Schrock of Cape Cod, MA)

WebQuests are a form of problem-based learning unit that uses similar elements described herein involving students using Web-based resources. As of this writing one of the best resources for such units is the Manteno Community Unit School District's (2006) WebQuest Web page. This site features WebQuests at all levels of schooling. See also the above two teacher resource sites.

LONG-TERM INQUIRY STRATEGIES

A long-term inquiry strategy is a set of learning experiences that, over time, engages students in identifying questions worth pursuing, researching, analyzing, and reporting the findings. Therefore, a strategy is a long-range plan, a series of logically connected episodes leading toward the resolution of some curiosity or issue.

The strategy will have these elements:

- An introductory experience, perhaps a problematic scenario that invites students to think and raise questions about the subject
- Core experiences involving students' organizing investigations and teacher-led discussions and lessons
- Culminating/assessment experiences involving final reports, projects, and other forms of formal and informal assessments

Any long-term strategy should also include planning for the following:

- Integrating thinking and inquiry processes (Levels II and III of Three-Story Intellect)
- Integrating social processes such as cooperative learning, sharing, listening, and responding as well as reflective practices
- Emphasizing key dispositions of habits of mind like inquisitiveness, risk taking, openness, empathy, and persistence

AUTHENTIC, ALTERNATIVE, PERFORMANCE ASSESSMENTS OF UNDERSTANDING

Testing, according to Wiggins (1993), is a process of

> taking complex performances and dividing them into discrete, independent tasks that minimize the ambiguity of the result. . . . As a result most tests tend to be indirect (and thereby inauthentic) ways of evaluating performances because tests must simplify each task in order to make items and answers unambiguous. (p. 15)

Assessment, on the other hand, is a long-term process of determining the depth and quality of students' understanding of concepts, ideas, and principles. Such measures can be very traditional, involving final examinations and written reports. With "authentic" assessment and achievement (Newmann & Associates, 1996; Wiggins, 1993) we emphasize using complex intellectual processes found in life experiences (e.g., problem solving, critical analysis, and decision making) to ensure students understand content and can apply learning to life beyond the classroom. Assessment is "authentic" if it involves students "in the general forms of cognitive work found in the adult world" (Newmann & Associates, 1996, p. 24).

Such cognitive work, reflected in the intellectual challenges of Levels II and III of the Three-Story Intellect, lead to students' gaining deeper understanding of what they are learning.

This will involve a wide variety of alternative assessment experiences, including formal reports, simulations, panel discussions, film making, creative projects, interviews, dramatizations, and the like, where we stress students' performing their understandings (Barell, 1995; Perkins, 1992).

Thus, when planning units of instruction we think up front about what it is we want students to be able to do and how we—and they—will determine the depth and quality of understanding.

EXAMPLE OF THE CURRICULUM PROCESS

All of these curricular elements are found within Jane Rowe's fifth-grade classroom (Provincetown Elementary School, Provincetown, MA) where students extensively research the problem of "Who Discovered America?" using artifacts and historical accounts. The class then shares their conclusions with a wider audience. The question arose from Jane's presenting students with many different clues (some over summer vacation) that created for them a curious, intriguing problem. How did the clues relate? What did they mean? Students then analyze the clues and arrive at the focus or essential question for the introductory unit of instruction. For this they have to think of the major ideas, or content, to present, analyze, and discuss. Jane helps students work toward specific intended outcomes, or objectives, such as drawing conclusions for themselves of historical importance based on a careful scrutiny of existing information.

Jane's long-range strategy is one of questioning and inquiring to answer the original question, and she uses individual and small group researching activities. Students use all sorts of resources: some original artifacts (or copies thereof), various writings of historians, and the like.

Finally, Jane has her students present their findings in the form of written conclusions shared with the entire class and the community. These assessment performances demonstrate to Jane the depth and quality of students' understanding of the ideas and critical thinking research skills. For example, the students judge the reliability of their sources, and Jane assesses their ability to draw reasonable conclusions.

Jane executes all the major elements of the curriculum process: a complex, robust situation that calls for inquiry, content of ideas and concepts, objectives, long-range strategies, resources, and performance assessments. These elements are found within every model of PBL (see Figure 3.1).

UNIT INSTRUCTION

Jane Rowe's strategy is one way of organizing unit instruction. It probably differs from what many teachers are used to. "Units?" some say, "We just teach chapter by chapter from the book." That's fine if the books are well organized, focus on key ideas and concepts, and foster important skills such as inquiring, problem posing and resolving, critical thinking, and reflecting.

Units provide a well-organized approach to instruction. They help ensure that all the various activities add up to meaningful learnings in which what

CURRICULUM PROCESS

Fill in the following for a unit of study:

Content

State Curriculum Content Standards

Objectives

Complex, Robust Situation/Problems Worth Investigating

Resources (People, Internet, Books, etc.)

Strategies (Teacher-Directed Inquiry, KWHLAQ, Observe-Think-Question, Independent Study)

Authentic, Alternative, Performance Assessments

Figure 3.1

is studied relates to what is already known. Inquiry can provide continuity for instruction, a "thread" running through units to help students organize the relationship between units. Units should organize lesson plans, not vice versa.

Thus, thinking ahead about which concepts, ideas, and principles engage students in thinking, doing, and feeling is one way for teachers to ensure that their instruction is meaningful to students. What teachers want to avoid is what Perkins (personal communication, July 1992) calls "Macbeth activities": many exciting, unrelated learning experiences, "full of sound and fury signifying nothing."

Without such organization, teachers may introduce students to some interesting experiences that they will remember, but will students be able to use the knowledge, skills, and dispositions in a meaningful way? A community of inquiry allows more opportunities for students to exercise more control over their own learning than in the traditional kind of classroom where the teacher plays the role of disseminator of information and evaluator of learning in the classroom.

Stop and Think

 What do you think contributes to meaningful learning?

The following contribute to meaningful learning:

- Student-initiated inquiry involves students responding to their own curiosities, not always the teacher's; they may have more of an investment (a "buy in") with their own questions
- Students making some choices about what to study and how
- Students' working with information, analyzing it, and solving problems fosters long-term recall of knowledge, over a longer period of time than just listening, remembering, and reciting information
- Students' constructing their own meanings, not merely copying those of the teacher, involves designing, making connections, finding relationships, and searching for patterns
- Students working collaboratively, listening and responding and learning from each other as adults do
- Students' and teachers' responding to presentations from students, giving and receiving important and direct feedback
- Students' responding to content in ways that may reflect their own learning style and interests as well as special needs; we all learn in different ways and that means affording *all* students choices in how they act upon content and make it meaningful

WHO'S IN CHARGE?

Obviously, teachers are always in charge, but an important issue in any inquiry or problem-based approach is deciding who controls the important curricular and instructional decisions and who makes the decisions about what, when, and how to study. Usually, teachers make these decisions, but if they really want students to feel comfortable asking good questions and posing problems that they can then solve, teachers need to alter this pattern of teachers' total control. Teachers can no longer make all of these curricular and instructional decisions. Here is a spectrum of control patterns:

Teacher Control	Shared Student-Teacher Control	Student Control
Teacher makes most decisions	Teacher and students share decision making	Students work more independently

Elements teachers can share with their students are the following:

Objectives: What do students want to study? What questions do they want to answer? What do they intend to learn?

Strategies: How will the students find the answers? How will they conduct research?

Resources: Who and what will help the students gather the knowledge they need? How will they process and apply it?

Assessments: How will students report their learnings? Who will set the criteria? What kinds of feedback will students want?

Reflection: How will students look back at what they have done, individually and cooperatively? How will they analyze their learnings, feelings, and new questions?

SUGGESTIONS FOR STARTING SMALL

How do teachers begin to share control over the elements mentioned above? At first, the best way to start is in small steps. What is known about successful change in schools suggests that teachers consider starting with incremental steps.

One way to begin the change process is by insisting everyone implement the innovation at the same time. Some research (Louis & Miles, 1990) supports this approach provided that leadership supports teachers with extensive resources. Another approach that seems more in line with the psychological need to proceed slowly and more comfortably, suggests that teachers take small steps, try them out, and observe the results. The following are some tested-in-the-classroom approaches teachers might try.

K-W-L

Use a K-W-L (Olge, 1986) strategy when introducing any short reading (see Figure 3.2):

K   What do we already **Know** about the topic? What do we *think* we know?

W   What do we **Want** to find out about the topic?

L   What have we **Learned** about the topic after reading?

Teachers and students can work either together or independently to fill in a K-W-L Chart. This strategy was designed to give students some control over their own reading processes; it has many benefits built into it.

Teachers learn what students already know. This might involve accurate conceptions as well as certain misconceptions; thus, it provides teachers with a wonderful initial assessment.

When teachers ask students to identify what they are curious about, teachers give students a sense of ownership. Students then have a purpose for reading, a stake in what's going on, and this can be a nearly revolutionary undertaking for some students.

When teachers conclude by asking students what they have learned, teachers afford students opportunities to organize their learning, alter misconceptions, transfer learning to other subjects, and generate some new questions. The spiral can be never ending—teachers can create a "thread" of inquiry on just this small scale.

THINKING/INQUIRY JOURNALS

As we mentioned above, it is a good idea to start recording and reflecting upon our own problem-solving and inquiry processes. We need to know how we approach complex situations like elections, planning trips and family occasions, breakdowns in appliances, or problems around the house. Being able to model for students how we identify and resolve problems will be an important first step in helping them do the same. Knowing what kinds of questions we ask will help us grow and model for our students what thinking is like in the adult world. Teachers' saying, "What I'm learning about my own thinking, problem solving, and questioning" will be an important first step in our curriculum development processes.

Following our own modeling, we can introduce Thinking/Inquiry Journals with stems such as the ones listed in Figure 3.3.

Teachers can use journals to clear up misunderstandings during class discussions and to redirect their efforts toward what students find difficult and what they are curious about. When using these kinds of journals, teachers are amazed that students' curiosities and confusions are not what they would have predicted. It's difficult for teachers to identify beforehand what students will find complex, confusing, and just too difficult to understand at any given time.

K-W-L CHART

What We **K**now	What We **W**ant to Find Out	What Have We **L**earned

Figure 3.2

SENTENCE STEMS FOR THINKING/INQUIRY JOURNALS

What I wonder about now is. . . .

What this means to me is. . . .

This reminds me of (other ideas, concepts, experiences). . . .

What is important here is. . . .

I feel. . . .

What I'm learning is. . . .

How this relates to my own experience. . . .

Figure 3.3

For example, one seventh-grade student recently discovered that the Venus flytrap captures insects that hit on its leaf hairs in very precise patterns (twice on one hair or once on two separate hairs). This student wondered, "Does this mean the plant is mathematical? Can it understand numbers?"

Having students make a journal entry for each chapter gives teachers the opportunity to see how willing students are to reveal their curiosities as well as their confusions. Here is where the community of inquiry and the invitational environment play a significant role.

QUALITY RESPONDING

Teachers can experiment on a small scale just in the way they respond to students' answers (see "Teachers' Quality Responding" in Chapter 2). For example, when teachers ask students to elaborate, to expand on their ideas, to respond to another student's ideas, they can also follow up with the kinds of questions in Figure 3.4.

These quality responding skills, asking students to elaborate, to develop, to relate, and to question (see Chapter 2), are what foster healthy inquiry and discussion in the classroom. These are skills teachers practice as they facilitate student discussions.

FACTOIDS AND CHARACTER DESCRIPTIONS

Another way of starting small is with a factoid, one fact that is full of meaning and can lead to fascinating inquiries and discussions. Consider a teacher who throws out this factoid: "Thomas Jefferson owned slaves." To engage students, the teacher might use a version of the Observe, Think, and Question approach outlined in Chapter 1: first Observe—What do you notice about this statement? What does it mean to you? Then What does it make you think of? What connections can you make? And, finally, What questions come to mind? For example, we might have these kinds of questions:

How do we know Jefferson owned slaves?

What were the reasons/consequences of Jefferson's owning slaves?

How did his ownership compare with that of others, like George Washington?

How could he do this and write about men being free in the Declaration of Independence?

It may take a while for students to get over their accustomed passivity with facts. After years and years of merely memorizing them, students need teacher modeling and lots of patient practice to turn out good questions.

Another good way to encourage students to take control of their learning is to start with a reading selection from a novel and elicit their thoughts. For

QUALITY RESPONDING QUESTIONS

What do you wonder about now?

Does this suggest any new approaches, ideas to you worth investigating?

What kinds of connections and relationships are becoming evident to you now?

Where should/need we go from here?

Figure 3.4

example, a teacher reads the following passage to students, which reveals much about a character:

> The boys and the girls live in separate worlds. The boys in their universe and we in ours.
>
> My brothers for example. They've got plenty to say to me and Nenny inside the house. But outside they can't be seen talking to girls. Carlos and Kiki are each other's best friend . . . not ours.
>
> Nenny is too young to be my friend. She's just my sister and that was not my fault. You don't pick your sisters, you just get them and sometimes they come like Nenny.
>
> She can't play with those Vargas kids or she'll turn out just like them. And since she comes right after me, she is my responsibility.
>
> Some day I will have a best friend all my own. One I can tell my secrets to. One who will understand my jokes without my having to explain them. Until then I am a red balloon, a balloon tied to an anchor. (Cisneros, 1989, pp. 8–9)

Afterward, the teacher engages the students by asking questions, such as the ones in Figure 3.5.

Stop and Think

 What factoids worth analyzing can you list from your own subject area? Share them with a partner to see what kinds of questions he or she can generate. Which ones would generate the greatest amount of good discussion?

SCIENCE EXPERIMENT

Any science experiment can be used to help students confront the strange, the complex, and the unusual. For example, a teacher can bring in five different kinds of apples and a bucket of water (or cans of regular and diet soda). Then the teacher can hold up each apple and ask students to predict whether it will float or sink and give good reasons. After students make predictions, the teacher can drop the different apples into the water, and then challenge students to observe results and pose questions or hypotheses to explain their observations. Students can use formats, such as the one in Figure 3.6, to record their findings.

LONG-RANGE VIEW: CURRICULAR MANAGEMENT AND STUDENTS WITH SPECIAL NEEDS

If teachers want to plan over a slightly longer period of time, they can follow the lead of one teacher who realized there wasn't sufficient time to engage

QUESTIONS FOR FACTOIDS AND CHARACTER DESCRIPTIONS

What does it mean to you?

What are the key elements/causes/consequences here?

What does it make you think of? What connections and relationships do you see? Please explain the similarities and differences.

What questions do you have now?

Figure 3.5

SCIENCE EXPERIMENT RECORD

Predictions (include reasoning):

Observations:

Questions:

Hypotheses:

Results of experiments (include what you've learned):

Figure 3.6

students in thinking productively about all the concepts in the remaining chapters of the earth science text. Herb Reinert (Dumont High School, Dumont, NJ) challenged his students to find a topic within the remaining chapters of the text, to pose one or more questions, to conduct research, and to share findings with the whole class. Some students, for example, chose to find out how hurricanes and tornadoes form, and what they can do to protect themselves against such natural disasters.

This strategy (which might be called "giving students free rein over a few well-selected topics") can be used at the end of a term when students have given sufficient evidence they can work well together and/or can pursue research individually.

Giving students these kinds of opportunities to pose their own questions about intriguing topics served another purpose: encouraging students to use their preferred learning and reporting styles.

Interestingly, this PBL approach seemed to work quite well for students with learning challenges. Two boys I observed did a report—accompanied by a homemade video—of tornadoes that demonstrated that they understood the meteorological conditions that caused them and the effects of their sweeping across the land. When I asked how they got so involved, one said, "I don't like sitting and listening. I work better with my hands." I wondered then how many "unclassified students" felt the same way!

Here is where PBL plays a very special role: affording all students, not just the gifted, opportunities to engage content in ways that are more meaningful and enjoyable for them than sitting, listening, and giving back all the information they've memorized.

I have used the term "boundaryless" (see Figure 4.3 in Chapter 4) to describe the problematic situation within a PBL unit and it applies here (Welch, 2001). Students can enter the content at varied points of interest and respond in ways of their own choosing, thus tearing down some of the traditional boundaries of how students learn in a traditional classroom. Students with special needs can enter and respond to complex problematic situations in many ways, some of which might reflect Gardner's multiple intelligences: different ways of learning and alternatives to the traditional read, recite, and report.

ASSESSMENT

An alternative to traditional methods of evaluation in which the teacher makes up all the questions, many of which demand recall of information, is to challenge students to make up their own examination questions. For example, teachers can give students an opportunity to write some good examination questions for any unit of instruction—about quilts, immigration, the solar system, and time and distance problems. For example, when teaching the novel *Crime and Punishment* I asked students to write examination questions and to create their own criteria for selecting several good ones. Two such questions were, "What do you think Dostoyevsky meant by including all the references to

Lazarus?" and, "If you were Raskolnikov, how would you have responded to the detective's persistent questioning?"

Students' Self-Assessment

Giving students an opportunity to reflect on their own learning as formative and summative assessments is a key self-direction approach to learning. Using Thinking Journals, students will share what they are learning about the subject and about their own problem-solving and inquiry processes:

1. "I'm learning that my early questions lead to many more."

2. "My thinking wasn't good because I just copied other peoples iders [*sic*]."

3. "If I persist, I can usually find answers to my questions."

Here are several other ways students can self-assess and reveal the depths of their understandings:

1. Concept Maps: "What do I think I know about the subject?" Use them at the beginning, middle, and at the end of a unit.

2. Folders and Portfolios: students periodically reflect on these during the year and use to set personal improvement goals.

3. Letters home to Mom and Dad to explain what students are learning.

We want to foster students' self-assessment for the simple reason that when they leave school, they're on their own, in command of their own learning processes.

Stop and Think

 What other ways have you tried or considered that afford students an opportunity to become more self-directed inquirers, more in control of their own learning?

Reflect on a lesson in which you presented students with opportunities for inquiry. What did you observe about their ability to formulate questions and pursue an inquiry strategy? What do you think they need to get better at?

What's My Thinking Now

Reflection

Comments

Questions

PART 2

Application

CHAPTER 4

Teacher-Directed Inquiry

HOW TO BEGIN PBL

Initiating PBL (problem-based learning) can be like preparing a meal for company. If people are having guests over to enjoy an invitational environment, they want to make sure that their meal is successful, enjoyable, and of course delicious! So most people would probably start with some dishes they have enjoyed before, food preparations with which they are familiar. They would think of all the meals they have prepared for themselves, identify those that they enjoyed the most, and decide which one would be most suitable to serve to guests. They would skip the pasta that gave Uncle Dan heartburn and avoid the roast that brought Sister Kate to paroxysms of laughter because it fell apart before being served.

Similar to preparing a meal, the easiest way for teachers to begin engaging students in PBL is to start with what they know best: teacher-directed inquiry. All teachers are familiar with making the crucial decisions in terms of what and how to study. They have all had years of experience selecting significant content concepts, ideas, and skills for students to become familiar with and to master. Therefore, it makes sense for teachers to start where they are the most comfortable.

By starting with what is familiar, comfortable, and somewhat predictable in terms of students' thinking and responses, teachers can begin with what they are sure of: a unit of instruction they have taught several times. Within a familiar subject, it's easier for teachers to identify elements that can become problematic situations for students.

MODELS FOR TEACHER-DIRECTED INSTRUCTION

Like the different combinations of spices and ingredients in cooking, there are different ways to engage students in thinking through problematic situations. These models represent three different approaches:

You are . . . statements place students in complex situations and ask them to play a role requiring problem solving.

What if . . . ? questions encourage students to respond to compelling hypothetical situations.

A **specific claim or judgment** elicits students' responses to a particular viewpoint.

These models offer three ways of organizing thinking about how to confront students with complex situations. For example, a couple is preparing a meal for about fifty people because their son or daughter is getting married. The couple is having the meal catered, and all the arrangements have been made. These are some of the problematic situations that teachers could have students work through:

You are in charge of all floral arrangements, the band, ushers, and sundry items. How would you organize these arrangements?

What if the caterer suddenly quits two days before the wedding in an argument with your spouse over the ingredients of the cake? What would you do?

After the caterer quits, a neighbor **concludes/claims**, "The best thing for you to do now is to postpone the wedding, give yourself two months and start over." Do you agree/disagree? Why?

Before teachers try to tackle these models in PBL, they need to organize their thinking. Gourmet chefs do not march blindly through a set of procedures, and neither should teachers. The following section includes a list of steps teachers might consider when designing a unit.

PROCESS FOR CREATING UNIT PLANS

Now how can teachers proceed? Teachers need to create a structure for the You are . . . , What if . . . ? and claim/judgment kinds of problematic situations. One way to create such a structure is to use the curricular concepts (see Chapter 3): identify content ideas and concepts worth thinking about; map them out to figure out what is important to teach; identify objectives, resources, strategies, and assessment experiences. These concepts provide teachers with a framework that guards against just planning some exciting events that add up to nothing significant, those "Macbeth Activities," as Perkins (personal communication, July 1992) calls them, "full of sound and fury signifying nothing!"

Ten Steps

Ten suggested ways for teachers to identify what they think is worth students' spending a lot of time thinking productively about are presented below.

Step One: Select a topic

Use existing curriculum, state curriculum content standards, textbooks, students' interests, and developmental levels as guiding criteria. Sometimes we have little choice, but on other occasions we can steer instruction more toward students' interests and/or pressing societal issues that will galvanize students' participation.

Step Two: Map out all possible elements of the topic

Brainstorm all possible elements of the topic that we might wish to incorporate within the unit. Here it's helpful to use a graphic organizer, such as a concept map. This is a most important step, especially if we are going to encourage students to pose questions they will want to investigate. If we have mapped out all possible elements of the topic, we can orient students' interests and questions within a larger conceptual framework for the unit.

Step Three: Decide which elements to include

Choose the elements from the mapped out topic to include in the unit using criteria similar to Step One: necessary to meet content standards; important to understand the major concept; appropriate for age/developmental levels of students; what students will find fascinating and lead to many questions worth investigating.

Step Four: Decide on the objectives

These *must* include challenges for students to gather information, to analyze it, to achieve understanding, and then to use it (see the Three-Story Intellect, Figure 2.3, for Levels II and III intellectual challenges as well as your state content standards). Objectives need to challenge students to think productively and not merely regurgitate information, as illustrated in Chapter 3.

Step Five: Identify essential questions or a problematic situation

Use the "You are a member of [a town planning committee, e.g.]" or "What if . . . ?" framework or make a claim or judgment that students can relate to on a direct, experiential level. Here we need to find or identify a complex, problematic situation (perhaps identified in the concept mapping process) that reflects the major concepts and ideas within the unit. For example, "You are responsible for ensuring clean water for your home town . . ." involves learning about the nature of clean water, conservation, pollution, effective health policies, civic responsibilities, and much more.

Step Six: Determine assessment learning experiences

It may be helpful to consider your problematic scenario as one of several summative assessment experiences.

Formulate formal and informal assessments wherein students demonstrate the depth and quality of their understanding of key concepts and ideas. Consider

Newmann's definition of "authentic achievement" as involving "cognitive work found in the adult world . . . organize, synthesize, interpret, explain, evaluate complex information in addressing a concept, problem or issue" (Newmann & Associates, 1996, pp. 24, 29). Assessments will, of course, be determined mostly by our objectives—what we want students to be able to know, be, and do at conclusion of the unit and that can incorporate the original problematic scenario—"You are a member of a committee charged with. . . ."

But we will also take time to listen to what students think is important, what they find fascinating, and what they're curious about.

Step Seven: Design long-term strategies

Use a framework of specific initial, core, and culminating experiences that challenge students to confront complex problematic situations, generate questions, conduct research, think critically about findings, and draw reasonable conclusions. Strategies will use varieties of group/individual investigations of varieties of resources, thinking critically about information acquired, sharing information, reporting, and reflecting on the process.

Step Eight: Create learning experiences

Plan weekly and daily learning experiences in accordance with learning objectives, ones that challenge students to recognize problems, learn how to generate questions, search for answers, and think critically about information, especially on the World Wide Web. Lessons will also focus upon key concepts to be learned.

Step Nine: Both students and teachers reflect on the process

Using discussions, Thinking Journals, interviews, and other means we ask, "What did I/we learn about the subject? About myself/ourselves? About working with others? About reasoning in the subject matter? What new questions do I/we have now?"

Step Ten: Provide opportunities for transfer and application

Encourage students to transfer/apply learnings from this unit to other topics studied, to other subjects, as well as to their lives beyond school. Here is where we ensure a depth of understanding of major concepts and skills.

CURRICULAR CONCEPTS

As discussed in Chapter 3, the following is an outline of the curricular concepts that help create structure:

> **Content:** Those concepts, ideas, principles, and skills that form the heart of the unit (e.g., mountain ranges, change/patterns, heroes/heroines, solving quadratic equations, etc.)

Objectives: What teachers specifically want students to do (the intellectual processes found on Levels II and III of Three-Story Intellect) during the unit, not what the teacher will say or do

Problematic Situations: Conflicts, difficulties, or puzzles teachers present to students for them to analyze, question, search for answers/solutions to, and to think critically about findings

Resources: Human, print, and media helpers for the unit

Strategies: Long-range plans that challenge students to pose and resolve problems, think critically, design new products or art works, hypothesize, design, and experiment

Assessment: Designing means of determining the depth and quality of students' understanding of major curricular concepts, ideas, and skills

SAMPLE UNITS[1]

The following are three examples illustrating the process of creating unit plans. They are accounts of three teachers as they prepare units of instruction at the elementary, middle, and high school levels. Anne Marie, Paul, and Jennifer are composites of actual teachers who have created such units. The first sample works step by step through Anne Marie's elementary school unit in an attempt to model the decision-making process suggested in the ten steps above, a process that incorporates all of the curricular elements, such as content, objectives, and problematic situations. The next two samples present in shorter form Paul's middle school unit and Jennifer's high school unit.

Anne Marie/Elementary School: Mountain Regions of the Eastern United States

Paul/Middle School: Ecology

Jennifer/High School: Literature

Each unit exemplifies one or more of the three problematic suggestions: You are. . . . , What if. . . . ?, and making a claim or judgment. It becomes obvious that teachers can use any one or more of these situations. The idea in using them is to personalize the problem to help students relate it to their own experience.

Sample Unit: Mountain Regions of the Eastern United States

Grade level: Elementary School

Model: You are. . . .

Anne Marie is teaching a combination of fourth and fifth grades, and she is interested in working on a more challenging unit with her students, who are very curious and love to work together. She wants to work on mountain regions of the eastern United States, specifically the Appalachian region, and has decided that this unit will look at the region from more than one point of view—perhaps culture and science.

Step One: Select a topic

How did she decide on this topic? Some teachers go right for the textbook and say, "Well, Chapter 4 discusses westward expansion (or the solar system), so that's what we have to do." That's fine; nothing in this book suggests that teachers must look outside of the accepted curriculum to engage students in problem solving. However, other teachers will think about what their students find fascinating and challenging: for example, whales, personal relationships, or heredity. Student interests, concerns, and needs are always important considerations; however, they give rise to a tension felt by all who design curricula, between what teachers are supposed to cover and what students would find more related to their own lives.

Anne Marie has selected mountain regions of the eastern United States for several reasons:

1. Her state standards call for understanding various concepts within earth science: earth systems and history, plate tectonics, mountain building forces, and the three basic kinds of rocks. These topics are also in her science textbook.

2. She knows that students in the past have had fun speculating about differences between the Appalachian and Rocky Mountains. They would also enjoy reading about cultures different from their own, because they are fascinated by how people live differently in other parts of the world.

3. This topic is current (in the news) because of recent stories about economic conditions and the culture of people living in the region.

Step Two: Map out all possible elements of the topic

One way for Anne Marie to approach this complex topic is to map out the possible areas that she might investigate during a unit. A good way to do this is to use a concept map to identify areas of potential study.

Anne Marie graphically charts out all of the associations she can make with this topic. She asks herself, "What do I know about the topic? What seems relevant and related? What ideas come from science, literature, art, anthropology/cultural studies, foreign languages, and physical education?"

She lets her mind cover the vast range of possibilities, because all she is concerned with now is identifying possible areas of study.

At this point, she is not worried that something might not be appropriate for her students in terms of interest or developmental ability. It's important for her to get her ideas down on paper (see Figure 4.1).

Figure 4.1   Concept Map of Appalachian Regions

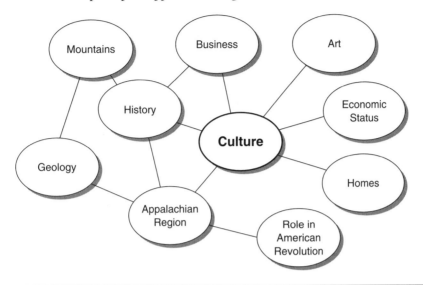

Stop and Think

Create a concept map for the Appalachian Mountains region or one for your own unit of study. Once you have identified as many different, possible areas of interest, determine which ones you think you would select for your unit. Think of what is important enough to spend several weeks on—what is in your state content curriculum standards.

Step Three: Decide which elements to include

Anne Marie now needs to decide which subtopics to include within her course of study. Here are some things for her to consider:

What do state content curriculum standards require? Consider both the curricular concepts, such as earth systems, history, and plate tectonics, as well as the ways of knowing important in science: asking questions, generating hypotheses, designing/implementing experiments, thinking critically, and the like. Most states have this information on their own Web sites (do a Google search for State Curriculum Standards). Additional information can also be found online; see Mid-continent Research for Education and Learning (McREL, n.d.) and the National Education Association (2006).

What topics are important for understanding the subject? This might be more important at the upper grade levels, especially in high school. Which concepts are important to understanding the subject matter in general and to understanding other key concepts and ideas? For example, including plate tectonics in a unit on mountains would help future understandings of the geological processes evident in the formation of the earth. Which have historical

significance? Anne Marie also considers which concepts are transferable to other subjects.

What interests students? Which areas will connect with students' interests and curiosities? This depends on the students, their background, and their age group. It is very important to select areas that can be related to students' lives in some way. This is not the only criterion, but it is the one that contributes so much to students' understanding the content of the instruction. When students can make connections to their lives (their thoughts/prior knowledge and current feelings and dispositions) and when they can see relationships between school content and themselves, it becomes more meaningful personally (Barell, 1995; Perkins, 1992). As McCarthy (1987) notes,

> Teachers as well as students need to understand the reasons for doing what they do. . . . We must answer the question "Why?" or no real learning can occur. We must create a desire, a desire that is there, within them. (p. 94)

This is an appeal to students' internal drives and interests as a curricular planning strategy.

Which topics have societal interest? For example, Anne Marie might want to include as a subtopic the issues such as equal access to educational and financial opportunities because they are real concerns in society at large.

These are four criteria for selecting topics for units of study (Barell, 1995). Using these criteria, Anne Marie decides on the following elements for her unit on the Appalachian Mountains region:

- How people live: work, school, art, religion, music (all students can relate to cultural concerns)
- Geology and geography: plate tectonics and mountain formation (these are important for future units in physical sciences)
- Economic conditions: important for concerns of personal and social relevance
- History: important within the larger scope of U.S. history and of personal interest to some students

Step Four: Decide on the objectives

Now Anne Marie must identify the objectives for her students. What should the students be able to do with these ideas by the end of the unit? Here she might think of the concepts she wants to focus on and the intellectual processes students will engage in. Anne Marie decides her content/concept ideas will be mountain building and cultural differences.

These are the two subtopics Anne Marie is including. Now what does she want students to be able to do with them? Her first thought is that she wants them to know what causes mountains to grow and to be able to tell how cultures are different. These objectives are fine. They include two of the major goals of education: retain information and understand it.

Stop and Think

If you look at the Three-Story Intellect (see Figure 2.3), you can determine for yourself what intellectual processes you might have students engage in. Look especially at Level II, the processing level, in which teachers engage students in thinking to deepen their understanding of a subject.

Anne Marie decides that she wants students to become better at analyzing situations on their own, figuring out what causes natural phenomena like mountain building, and determining how different cultures relate to each other. This means students will search for causes, engage in comparing and contrasting, and draw conclusions. The following are some of her objectives:

- Identify elements of a culture
- Compare students' culture with the region's and draw conclusions
- Analyze why people continue to live amid such difficult economic situations
- Determine how mountains form, compare Appalachian with Rocky Mountains, Cascades, and Himalayas, and draw conclusions using concepts of plate tectonics
- Design an artifact representative of the culture

Stop and Think

Now think of objectives you would use for students in this Appalachian unit or in your own unit of study. Consider content concepts and intellectual processes.

Step Five: Identify an essential question or problematic situation

Anne Marie now uses the concept map (see Figure 4.1) and/or the objectives to identify several problematic areas where there are doubts, difficulties, and uncertainties worthy of students' deep thought for a significant amount of time (from one week's lesson to much longer). One way for her to do this is to select an area of interest or apparent uncertainty and proceed to pose a number of questions about it, questions from her own curiosity or questions she thinks students might be interested in. Anne Marie can use the criteria in Figure 4.2 to assess the significance of the problematic situations.

Anne Marie might look in the economics area and see that there is intense poverty. She can discuss this with students and ask the following kinds of questions:

- Why do such conditions exist?
- How long have they lasted?

CRITERIA FOR PROBLEMATIC SITUATIONS

Complex: Many faceted, nonstructured, open to questions

Robust: Concepts are significant, central to understanding the subject

Fascinating: Arouses students' curiosity; relates to their needs, interests, or concerns

Researchable: Is there information available?

Significant to current concerns: Relates to significant social, political, historic, scientific issues

Transferable: Are concepts and skills applicable to other subjects or to life situations?

"Boundaryless": Transcends traditional lines of subject/authority, learning entry points, sharing, and reporting on conclusions

Figure 4.2

- What keeps people living in poverty?
- What would it take to alter these conditions?
- Are conditions in other mountain regions similar (e.g., Rockies, White Mountains, etc.)?

Notice that questions such as, "Why do people continue to live in the poverty of this region?" represent some kind of doubt or uncertainty; therefore, they might become good problematic situations for students to investigate. Sizer (1992) would call these "essential questions" that are important and can kindle inquiry. Thus, Anne Marie intends to start identifying problems by identifying those areas about which she is most curious (see Figure 4.3).

Now Anne Marie selects several areas from the concept map in Step Two (see Figure 4.1) and outlines some potential problematic areas:

Content Area: Geology and Geography

Possible Questions/Problems: Why do the Appalachian Mountains look different from the Rockies? the Alps?

Content Area: Culture

Figure 4.3 Examples of Problematic Situations

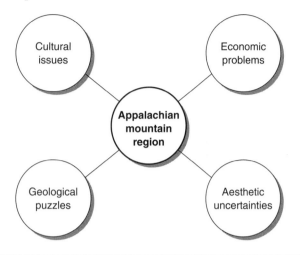

Possible Questions/Problems: How is the culture of the Appalachian people different from other mountain dwellers' cultures? Different from the students' culture?

Anne Marie selects geology and geography and culture for her content and asks herself if they meet her criteria (see Figure 4.4).

Stop and Think

Generate your own questions and identify which levels of the Three-Story Intellect (see Figure 2.3) you think they represent. What problematic situation would you present to your students for the Appalachian unit or your own unit of study?

Anne Marie has accomplished a lot! She has worked through what some teachers think is the most difficult part of curriculum planning, deciding what is worth thinking long and hard about and what teachers are willing to devote more than a week's worth of work to. Figures 4.5 and 4.6 represent Anne Marie's curriculum plan thus far.

Stop and Think

Now try to create a unit of your own, defining content, objectives, and possible problematic situations. Use Figure 4.7.

CRITERIA FOR CONTENT AREAS

Area Question	Yes	No
Geology and Geography		
Criteria	✓	
Complex	✓	
Robust	✓	
Fascinating	✓	
Researchable/answerable	✓	
Significant to social concerns	✓	
Transferable	✓	
Culture		
Criteria	✓	
Complex	✓	
Robust	✓	
Fascinating	✓	
Researchable/answerable	✓	
Significant to social concerns	✓	
Transferable	✓	

Figure 4.4

These are situations that Anne Marie might present to students at different times during instruction, and they are just like complex situations she has presented to her students in the past. It is important to note that if we commence a unit with a problematic scenario like B in Figure 4.5 ("You are a young economist. . . ."), then our assessments can and should include opportunities for students to complete this task, presenting reasoned conclusions about current economic conditions and alternative approaches to alleviating their impact upon people.

The possible problematic situations presented above demand of students certain kinds of intellectual processes. These intellectual processes, such as problem solving or creating, must be part of unit objectives. Teachers need to identify them specifically to ensure that they plan for specific learning experiences that will help students become more skillful in using them. If teachers want students to attempt to identify the problems associated with economic conditions and think of how to solve them, students must have experiences in problem identification and analysis, solution generation, decision making, implementing, and evaluating. Teachers cannot assume that students are skillful in all of the intellectual processes mentioned in the Three-Story Intellect (see Figure 2.3).

Figure 4.8   Concept Map of Long-Term Strategies

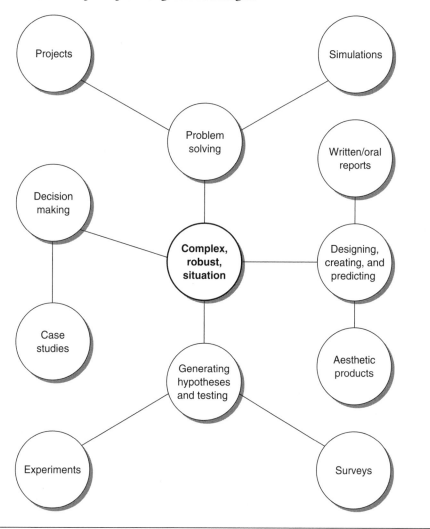

staying there and what they might do to alter their own situation. Here are some suggested experiences that might relate to this objective:

- Examining economic statistics
- Researching (Internet, books, magazines, etc.)
- Learning problem-solving strategies
- Interviewing people for information
- Reading stories about families
- Small group problem posing/resolving
- Viewing videos, CD-ROMs, or other media

One other strategic consideration that might help Anne Marie organize her learning experiences is to divide them up into beginning (initiating), middle (core), and ending (culminating) kinds of activities.

For example, she wants to commence her unit by grabbing students' attention and helping them see how they relate to the content. Making this kind

of connection is vital, as mentioned above, for students' motivation—for their buying into the ideas Anne Marie is thinking about. When students make connections with content they are making it meaningful for themselves.

Stop and Think

 The initiating experience must be carefully thought out. What are some possible learning experiences that would serve to hook students' interests, to help them see the relationships between the unit and their own lives, interest, curiosities, and prior knowledge?

Anne Marie might, for example, consider starting with the following versions of Observe, Think, and Question:

1. Two photos, one of the Appalachian Mountains and the other of the Rocky Mountains. The questions would be, "What do you notice here? What questions can you pose?"

2. Read a short story or a mini–case-study of a family living in the region. Ask students the following questions: What did you think was interesting in this story? What surprised, confused, or upset you? Why? How do the characters relate to you? What would you like to know now? What are you curious about?

3. Examine various cultural artifacts, some from Appalachia, some from students' own culture. Engage students in examining each objectively and then in attempting to figure out what kinds of cultural priorities/ values or ideas they might reflect. Ask students to formulate questions.

These initiating experiences might be the most important of the entire unit, for here is where Anne Marie hopes to tap into students' intrinsic motivations to give them an opportunity to connect with the subject matter and to create their own stake in the unit. This is why she provides them with an opportunity to pose questions of their own, questions that might provide Anne Marie with additional goals to work toward and provide students with some ownership of the unit.

Then Anne Marie moves on to the core learning experiences, in which students engage in those critical-thinking processes that lead toward deeper understanding of content. She wants students to investigate and gather information, then solve problems, analyze and debate issues, search for reasons, engage in experiments, and create new products.

Say, for example, that Anne Marie is working on the economic objective of determining what alternatives people in Appalachia might develop for themselves. In this middle, core phase of her unit she might want students to engage as follows:

- Form students into investigative teams to gather and analyze economic information about living conditions, jobs, and opportunities in the areas
- Use all available resources: Internet, CD-ROMs, encyclopedias, and other books
- Interview resource persons, some who are experts, some who might have lived in the area; make telephone inquiries or e-mail requests for information
- Spend time analyzing findings and begin to draw tentative conclusions

As mentioned in Chapter 1, it is during the research/investigation and reporting phases that PBL comes into full flower. Teachers—often with students' input—organize class time for investigations and lessons on various concepts, how to analyze information on the Web critically and how to avoid plagiarism (see Heidi Nyser's example in Chapter 3).

- Teachers facilitate students' investigations, taking into account their various learning styles, learning abilities, and challenges. Here is where we use Carol Ann Tomlinson's (1999) principles and practices to differentiate our classroom.
- Students work individually or in groups to gather information
- Students share resources and information
- Students reflect on what they originally thought about the subject, identifying new concerns and questions
- Students analyze findings, being careful to detect bias, differentiate fact from inference, and draw reasonable conclusions from supportive and representative evidence
- Students compile results, discuss significance/meaning of findings, and try to come to tentative conclusions
- Students plan how to share research findings and conclusions with others

Once students have gathered and processed information and gained a much deeper understanding of the situations in Appalachia than they could have from just reading a few paragraphs in the textbook, Anne Marie needs to provide a culminating experience. Here is where students share their ideas, engage in presenting conclusions, make presentations on findings, and so forth.

Stop and Think

 Given your objectives and the kinds of learning experiences explored above, how would you suggest students culminate their learning processes and demonstrate their understanding of the major ideas? As Perkins (1992) might say, "What are some performances of understanding that they can engage in?"

Here are some of the suggestions Anne Marie thought of:

- Panel discussions
- Written project reports
- Videos of living conditions/solutions
- Dramatic enactments of conditions/solutions

There are so many possibilities. If Anne Marie considers these as the ways in which students culminate their projects, she has many ideas that she has tried and has seen others engage in.

Step Eight: Determine assessment learning experiences

When Anne Marie wishes to evaluate her students' understanding of the content, she returns to her problematic scenario: "You are a young economist . . ." This scenario gives her a comprehensive introduction to the unit and offers a good assessment experience to students. She can also consider other alternative forms of assessment:

- Dramatize a concept/idea
- Create a problem and solve it
- Use any visual or plastic art form to illustrate understanding
- Create models, metaphors, analogies
- Produce panels, newscasts, slide presentations
- Maintain Thinking/Reflective Journals
- Dance an idea
- Hold a debate
- Make audio/video tapes
- Conduct interviews
- Create a story or musical composition illustrating a concept

Several ideas run through all of the above assessment opportunities. There are multiple ways in which students can demonstrate their understanding of important concepts and ideas, not just one (traditionally, a written form). What teachers usually find in art class (pictures), what they often find in language arts class (metaphors), and what they find in science class (models) are all excellent ways for their students' creative imaginations to express themselves.

Teachers might say that they are using alternative modes of representational competence to express their understandings. All of these assessments are ways students can represent what they understand, and teachers need to realize that they all possess these multiple ways of representing what they understand. Teachers represent through pictures, actions, words, symbols (such as the flag, musical notations), metaphors, and numbers.

The following are Anne Marie's objectives and ways for her to determine the levels of her students' understanding:

Objective A: Identify major geographical areas and figure out how mountains form

Assessment A: Present a project that illustrates how mountains form and in the oral presentation demonstrate understanding of different geological processes; compare Appalachian Mountains and Rockies to two other sets of mountains and draw conclusions about formation forces and processes

Objective B: Compare and contrast culture of Appalachian region and draw conclusions with respect to your own culture

Assessment B: Complete a written report/panel discussion

Objective C: Analyze the economic situation, develop alternatives, and make recommendations

Assessment C: Make a written/oral report to the Council of Economic Advisors of the president of the United States; assume you have power to implement one or more solutions. Which would you choose and why? (an original problematic scenario)

Objective D: Create an original work of art that reflects the Appalachian culture

Assessment D: Show and explain your thinking process for your work of art (it can be in any medium reflective of the region)

Stop and Think

 Can you think of other assessment ideas for these objectives? Can you think of alternative assessment ideas to use in your own unit of study?

A possible teacher assessment rubric might include these criteria:

Presentation Skills

Organization of Content

Knowledge and Understanding of Content

Critical Reasoning

Step Nine: Both students and teachers reflect on the process

Here the teacher asks students to reflect metacognitively on the whole process:

- What have we learned about geology? About culture?
- What have we learned about how scientists think?
- What have we learned about ourselves, especially about working together as researchers? As young scientists?
- What have we learned about our own thinking and feelings?

- What thinking strategies/processes were most valuable to us? (Here Anne Marie might elicit such processes as brainstorming, identifying the problem, generating solutions, weighing alternatives with pro/con lists, decision making, etc.)
- How well did you use these strategies? How well did you work together? How well did you conduct research? Did you make a plan and execute it well?
- What might you do differently next time? Why?
- What new questions do we have and how can we pursue consensus?

Anne Marie wants students to reflect on their own thinking and feelings to become more in control of their own learning. She wants her students to ask themselves these questions with the intention that they internalize them, so they become automatic when students engage in any kind of challenging task. Students in control of their own learning tend to achieve at higher levels (McCombs, 1991).

Step Ten: Provide opportunities for transfer and application

At this stage, the teacher asks students how they can use the major ideas and concepts or skills from this unit in other subjects or in their own lives beyond school. For example, here are some suggested ways of engaging students in transfer and application experiences:

Geological Concepts. Students have learned about how mountains form, about erosion, about plate tectonics, about movement of continents across the face of the earth, and perhaps about faults and earthquakes.

Possible Transfer Questions. Anne Marie can ask her students the following questions:

- How can you relate the concepts of erosion, plate tectonics, and earthquakes to any other subject we have studied?
- Where in your personal life does the concept of fault lines and erosion apply?
- How could the idea of continental drift be applied to human relations, to diplomacy with other countries, or to your own personal life? (For example, how do countries drift apart over time, how do your own situations slowly change and develop over the years?)

Possible Transfer Approaches

- Class discussion
- End of project analyses
- Thinking Journals

The idea here, as Perkins (Fogarty, Perkins, & Barell, 1992) would say, is to bridge the Appalachian Mountains experiences to other subjects and areas of students' lives. Why? Because creating these bridges contributes to the meaningfulness of the learning. The more connections Anne Marie can make between and among the students' learnings, the more significant they become. The more pathways Anne Marie establishes among concepts, ideas, principles, and facts, the more significant and perhaps useful they are to students. Finally, such transfer exercises give students another opportunity to share the depth and quality of their understanding.

Sample Unit: Ecology

Grade level: Middle School

Model: What if. . . ?

Paul's unit models another type of problematic situation: What if. . . ? Paul has already mapped out the content and objectives, now he needs to generate the problematic situations (see Figure 4.9). Paul's concept map focuses on preserving the environment. His analysis of this topic is broad, which affords him many possible problematic situations as well as objectives and strategies for problem solving and projects.

Now Paul must decide among all of the possible elements which ones his seventh and eighth graders can relate to, which ones will challenge them meaningfully. He chooses for his content the following topics:

- Causes of pollution
- Water, land, and air quality
- Alternatives to fossil fuels
- Effects on animals
- Major polluters
- Local environments and habitats

With all of these topics, Paul needs something to focus students' attention, a concept that will help organize the unit. Paul knows that some of his students are very active; they like to get involved in projects. Others are more quietly reflective. While some are very independent thinkers, others are more dependent on friends' and adults' thinking. Some students require concrete examples and clearly delineated structures that help organize instruction. Others are capable of more abstract reasoning, speculating, and imagining What if. . . ? kinds of possibilities. One of the advantages of PBL is that with its problematic scenarios it provides many and varied opportunities for students with different abilities, talents, and challenges to get involved.

Paul decides to focus on how to preserve local environments. This will encompass the nature of environments, what certain parties (like industries) are doing that spoils them, and how students can assume personal responsibility for making contributions.

Now Paul thinks about his objectives. He wants his students to engage in a long-term project. He figures that students must engage in some planning; they

Figure 4.9 Paul's Concept Map

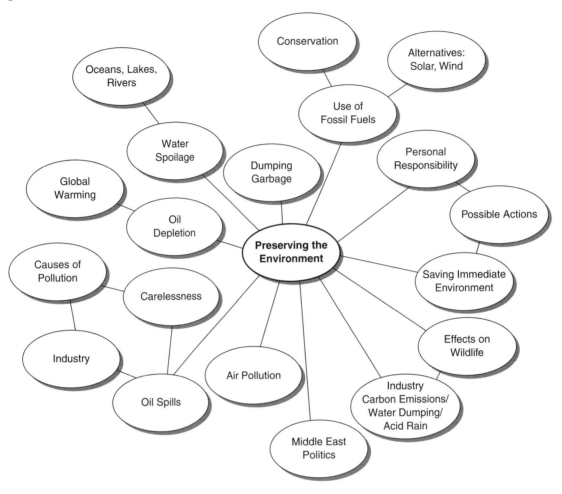

must figure out solutions to practice problem solving. He has noticed that sometimes his students impulsively jump to conclusions or agree with whomever speaks first or speaks with a sense of authority. He wants to help them get better at thinking independently through problems, but Paul also wants them to get better at working collaboratively. He has noticed that in the past some students are not good listeners while others take over the whole operation. The following are his objectives:

- Investigate and describe the nature of the global and local environments, especially the quality of air, water, and land
- Analyze the effects of global warming, ozone depletion, burning of fossil fuels, oil spillage on local or national environments
- Investigate and analyze the nature of animals' habitats (e.g., penguins in Antarctica, fish in eastern U.S. coastal waters)
- Engage in problem posing and resolving with the focus being on taking some personal responsibility for altering the local environment

- Improve the quality of group cooperative learning
- Raise questions about the environment and search for answers
- Be able to reflect on and analyze own and group problem-solving skills, draw conclusions, and set goals for improvement

Now Paul's task is to identify the kinds of problematic situations he wants his students to engage in. He considers many questions and finally settles on this as his essential question that will pose a problem: "How can we protect and preserve the local environment?"

Paul thinks, "OK, this is a good question, but how do I connect it with my students' lives?" One way is for him to imagine several possible problem situations that contain a What if. . . ? scenario. The following are some possibilities he considers:

A. Show students comparative vials of water: clear, bottled water and water from a local stream. What if you were a scientist? How would you analyze the contents for ingredients and impurities and draw conclusions?

B. What if there were a major oil spill in a harbor or lake near you. What courses of action would you suggest immediately? long term? What resource persons would you contact if you were the harbor master? a marine biologist? the EPA? a yacht owner with a boat in that harbor or lake? Support your conclusions and plan of action.

C. What if it was your job to examine monthly maps depicting the hole in the ozone layer as it shrinks and expands over the continent of Antarctica during the year? (Use Internet search engines like http://www.google.com and http://www.ask.com to search for Web sites about Antarctica; also see the National Science Foundation's Web site.) What do you notice about these maps? What do you think are the effects on persons and animals living under the widening hole? What might cause this depletion and what will happen if conditions continue to worsen? What can we do to minimize damage to humans, animals, and the environment?

D. What if an industry upstream from where you are announced they could no longer burn waste products. What would you think? What would you investigate? Why?

Each of these possible scenarios could serve as Paul's initiating experience: introducing students to the unit, providing them with an opportunity to connect the content to their lives, raising questions and setting the unit on a course of action—Paul's long-range strategy of inquiry and problem solving.

Let us not forget that each problematic scenario logically serves as at least one of the culminating projects for a means of assessing students' learning and depth of understanding of important concepts.

As Anne Marie did in the elementary school unit, Paul needs to consider what intellectual challenges he is presenting with each of the problematic situations.

Stop and Think

 Using the Three-Story Intellect (see Figure 2.3) as a guide, identify some of the major intellectual processes Paul might identify and include.

The following are the intellectual processes that Paul demands of his students with these problematic situations:

A. Compare and contrast, then draw conclusions based on evidence. Requires knowledge of water composition and effects of pollutants on water. This does not mean students must memorize the information first. They can begin their investigations of ecology by being puzzled by the comparison and the possible effects on our health of drinking water with little impurities floating around in it.

B. This is a very complex problem suitable for opening a unit on ecology. The problem raises so many questions about what to do that students can spend a major portion of the unit investigating water, effects of pollutants on water, or roles of various responsible individuals: EPA, local harbor masters, pilots and owners of ships, local oil companies, and so forth. This requires gathering a lot of information, analyzing it for its meaning, comparing actions and effects in the past (e.g., any oceanic oil spill or a more limited one like Alaska's Prince William Sound), and drawing up a new plan suitable for the circumstances using historical and environmental guidelines/criteria. (What are the elements of a good cleanup program? of a good prevention program?)

C. This requires knowledge of the effects of the sun on humans and animals, its beneficial and harmful rays. It requires some research on causes of ozone depletion and the extended length of time that CFCs (chlorofluorocarbons) stay in the air (about 75 years). Plans drawn up will have to take these seventy-five years into account and the current nature of the problem (e.g., is either China or India a current signatory to an international treaty calling for reduction of CFCs and/or participant in treaties like Kyoto to reduce industrial emissions?). This problem may also be suitable for a shorter term problem, say several days.

D. Not too much imaginative thinking is required to project oneself into the mind of an industrialist who, to save money, is no longer burning waste products and who has a quickly moving stream in his or her backyard. It calls for suggesting possibilities: They will dump the waste products, they will cease using certain pollution-creating elements, they will cease manufacture of the items in question. One other possibility is that there is a new technology designed to eliminate pollution-causing byproducts. Students will examine all possibilities, generate likelihood tables, and set up investigation plans to determine what is happening. This requires students to gather information and interpret it and then devise a course of possible, responsible community action, if necessary.

Paul's long-term strategies involve some of the major intellectual processes in Figure 4.9. Paul must include problem solving, of course, and he must provide students with these kinds of learning experiences:

- Modeling good problem-solving behavior (e.g., Paul does this using examples from his own life and from students' lives, both drawn from their Thinking Journal entries)
- Teaching what makes good problem solving, critical analysis of resource information, and how to draw reasonable conclusions
- Modeling good cooperative group work (e.g., direct teaching of such behaviors as listening, cooperating, overcoming impulsivity, etc.)
- Teaching basic science concepts directly and using textbooks, CD-ROMs, and Internet resources to gather information
- Teaching how to generate good questions (of texts, of persons being interviewed; what makes a good question?)
- Group investigations of ozone depletion, global warming, and uses of fossil fuels
- Class reflections on planning, monitoring of progress, writing in Thinking/Reflective Journals

These are just some of the learning experiences that help Paul guide students toward the goals he has outlined. Even though this is an example of a teacher-directed unit, there will be many questions that students can and will raise. Paul's focus is on making more of the decisions this time around. Later, students' questions will become more of a guiding force (see Chapter 5).

Paul must, in the end, provide culminating and assessment experiences. He decides to combine the two with experiences like the following, giving students some choices:

1. Make a report of your findings on the environment, including your recommendations for solutions to the problems. Present the report before an audience of twelfth graders for their feedback.

2. Do an investigative report on the status of a local body of water, identifying its condition and probable causes of any pollution found. Make recommendations that you will present to local authorities. Use audio- or videotapes and written reports.

3. All students: Create questions to be used on an essay examination, questions that cover all three levels of the Three-Story Intellect (see Figure 2.3). Provide all students with opportunities to respond using any text material available. Develop criteria for good responses and engage students in self-evaluation.

For transfer and application experiences, Paul decides to challenge students to do the following:

1. Use your Thinking/Reflection Journals to identify the concepts and skills you think are most generalizable to other subjects and areas of your lives.

2. Show how you could and will use the concepts and skills in one other subject and one area of your life. Demonstrate the application of new knowledge in and outside of school. This will be part of your presentation to the twelfth graders and their teachers.

Stop and Think

 What is your critique of Paul's unit? What are some positive elements? What are some areas where you think he might have difficulty? What alterations would you make given your own situation and why?

Sample Unit: Literature

Grade level: High School

Model: A Specific Claim or Judgment

This high school unit is taught by Jennifer, a language arts teacher. Jennifer teaches in a multiethnic school with students from many different cultural backgrounds. By and large students get along, but there are philosophical, cultural, and economic differences that spark serious debate and, unfortunately, occasional antisocial outbursts. Jennifer wants to engage her students in thinking constructively about human relationships, especially among persons of different ethnic backgrounds. She has enjoyed teaching such novels as *Black Boy*, *Snow Falling on Cedars*, *The Color Purple*, *Their Eyes Were Watching God*, and *The Joy Luck Club*. Jennifer wants to combine reading one or more of these texts with challenging her students to think about how they relate to each other in and out of the classroom. She would like them to think positively about how to work toward better understanding of different ethnic backgrounds through knowledge about cultural differences and histories. She maps out all her ideas (see Figure 4.10).

Looking at her map, Jennifer decides on the following major topics for her content:

1. How cultures differ with respect to education, social customs, religious beliefs, work/play

2. What causes stress between different cultures?

3. History of cultural disputes

4. How to deal positively with cultural differences

Figure 4.10   Jennifer's Concept Map

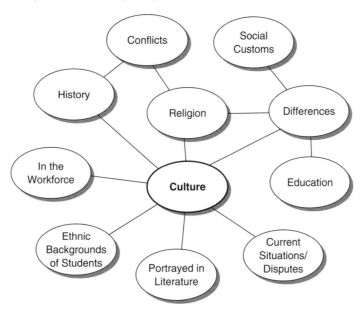

Then Jennifer considers her objectives (students will. . . .):

1. Analyze cultural confrontations in literature and give reasons for their existence

2. Relate these difficulties to the cultural backgrounds and histories of those involved, relate issues to their own cultural experiences, and draw conclusions

3. Use history and current problematic situations presented in life and literature, identify problems, generate possible solutions, retrospectively and currently, and make recommendations; become better problem solvers

4. Become better listeners to others' points of view

5. Be able to empathize and visualize the lives of those who are different

6. Maintain Reflective Journals that relate readings to students' own current experiences and draw conclusions

Jennifer's objectives suggest several problematic situations:

A. "Today's youngsters usually understand the points of view of others from very different backgrounds better than many adults." Do you agree with the statement? Why or why not?

B. "It is really not possible for people of different racial/ethnic/cultural backgrounds to live amicably together." Do you agree with the statement? Why or why not?

C. Consider the tensions in such places as the Middle East, Africa, and elsewhere. Do you agree with this statement: "It is best for people of similar backgrounds to live together, separate from those who are different."

D. "Literature can do a lot to help us understand people who are different." Do you agree with the statement? Why or why not?

Any one of these questions might lead Jennifer toward her major strategy for this unit: problem solving. Given the difficulties she sees in her school she really wants students to come to grips with the realities they face and attempt to understand their causes and potential solutions.

Jennifer considers her long-range strategy as problem posing and resolving, using literature as a resource to confront important issues. She reflects on some of these possibilities for her initiating experience:

1. Read a portion of one of the novels, for example, one depicting how white southerners treated Richard Wright during his boyhood working experiences, or how men and women from Washington state referred to their Japanese neighbors who worked the same land and fished the same waters (texts: *Black Boy* and *Snow Falling on Cedars*).

    a. Engage students in analyzing each situation. Identify what is occurring. Search for reasons. Examine likely feelings of the participants.

    b. Seek initial remedies.

2. Make the claim: "Situations like these occur only in literature." Apply general concepts and feelings to today's world.

Jennifer's core experiences logically include the following:

1. Have students read the assigned literature.

2. Divide students into reading teams with each team responsible for presenting the following for class discussion of major portions of the novels (e.g., chapters): Plot summaries, major conflicts therein, questions for discussion about plot, character, imagery, and themes, such as human relations differences and prospects for harmonious relationships. Here Jennifer will model different question stems.

3. Direct teaching of curricular concepts (e.g., culture, race, class, gender) as well as problem analysis, solution generation, and selection, decision making, action, and self-reflection.

4. Maintain Thinking/Reflective Journals relating literature actions, themes, and characters to one's own life.

Jennifer's culminating experiences include one or more of the following:

1. Form panels to create and dramatize cultural/racial conflicts for general class analysis and solutions.

2. Write a story involving different ethnic/racial groups in conflict with resolutions that illustrate your beliefs about how people can live together harmoniously (if you think they can).

3. Play the role of social historian and write about the conflicts in one of the novels. Describe the social tensions among groups and suggest viable solutions that include references to schools, businesses, families, and religious organizations.

These experiences serve as assessment experiences as well. For transfer and application experiences, Jennifer looks to students' Thinking/Reflective Journals:

1. Summarize all your entries and draw conclusions about the meanings for you and for the rest of society from the conflicts and solutions you have read about.

2. Show how the major ideas of the stories relate to your own experiences. How can they apply to your life in school, at home, and later in life?

With this kind of assignment Jennifer has also challenged her students to reflect metacognitively on their experience with this unit. Resource A, at the end of this book, offers alternative lessons in biology and history.

BENEFITS OF TEACHER-DIRECTED INSTRUCTION

In this chapter there are several examples of how to develop teacher-directed PBL units. Again, this means that teachers make most of the important decisions:

- Nature of Content and Objectives
- Problematic Situations
- Strategies
- Evaluation

It's best for teachers to begin with familiar units and topics, just as chefs begin with the meals they know are pleasing and delicious. It's important to think of the meals that, with a little dash of this and dollop of that, always have people pushing back from the table satiated and satisfied. Planning a PBL unit may take ten or more steps, but it always relies on teacher creativity and the teacher's ability to be flexible in challenging students to think productively.

Teacher-directed inquiry is a good way to start the beginning of the year. It gets students used to the idea of being challenged to think productively, to ask important questions in a risk-free, accepting and invitational environment, and to work collaboratively together.

Commencing with tight teacher control lays the groundwork for involving students in more of the planning later in the year.

NOTE

1. All names of educators and students have been changed.

What's My Thinking Now

Reflection

Comments

Questions

CHAPTER 5

Teacher-Student Shared Inquiry

SHARED DECISION-MAKING PROCESS

This exploration of PBL (problem-based learning) began in an area teachers feel most comfortable, with teacher-directed projects (see Chapter 4). Now the exploration moves to alternative curriculum units in which students have more say in their own education; that is, they share in some of the decision-making processes. With teacher-student shared inquiry, students begin identifying some of their curiosities, some of the questions they think are important and worth investigating.

Developing our sense of awe, wonder, and curiosity is very important for our growth as persons and as a civilization. Just listen to a character ("Mr.") from Alice Walker's searing novel, *The Color Purple:*

> I think us here to wonder . . . to ast. And that in wondering bout the big things and asting bout the big things, you learn about the little ones, almost by accident. But you never know nothing more about the big things than you start out with. The more I wonder . . . The more I love. (Walker 1982, p. 290)

The major strategy for this shared inquiry is one teachers can readily adapt to their own classroom, the KWHLAQ. This strategy is easy to identify and transfer to the content of just about any subject with any students. The letters stand for intellectual challenges: students identify what they Know and Want to know about a subject, decide How to find out, assess what they Learn and Apply it, and create new Questions. Sometimes teachers at various levels have said that their students don't really want to know anything; they aren't curious. Therefore, what students of any subject need to know to understand a specific problem is added to the concept. In other words, what questions does a thorough investigator—a professional—need to ask to understand this complex, strange phenomenon better?

The second strategy, called Observe-Think-Question (O-T-Q), derives from scientific investigation, or, for that matter, any thorough investigation of a situation. Teachers instruct students to observe phenomena closely, objectively, and precisely, to think reflectively about their observations, and then to

generate questions. This strategy is useful at all grade levels with objects and situations close at hand, from fossils to late-breaking news stories and can be used as initial experiences for students to become comfortable observing and asking questions. In other words, we can use O-T-Q (Observe, Think, and Question) as we are establishing the environment that invites students' questions, is supportive, and is risk-free.

WHEN IS A TEACHER READY?

How does a teacher know when it is appropriate to engage students in negotiated inquiry? When teachers can meet the following criteria, it's time to embark on teacher-student shared inquiry:

- Have plenty of experience with teacher-directed inquiry
- Feel comfortable about students' engaging in collaborative research
- Recognize that students possess the social skills to work together (i.e., they have learned how to act responsibly, listen, cooperate, think critically, and show a degree of self-direction appropriate for their age)
- Be assured that there are sufficient resources (Internet, library, personnel, etc.) to accomplish teacher's and students' goals
- Are willing to deal with varying amounts of ambiguity and students' generating questions and objectives that take off in unanticipated and unpredictable directions (if teachers like the excitement of seeing how curious students are and the new and different directions their inquisitiveness can take a class, then this might be for them!)

Does this mean that teachers are now sitting on the sidelines watching students think? Far from it! During these teacher-student negotiated units it is imperative for teachers to have mapped out their important curriculum priorities. See Step Two in Chapter 4. These priorities become the core objectives that everyone works toward (see Figure 5.1).

STRATEGIES

The strategies that form the core of the inquiry process can be used in two ways:

1. The KWHLAQ is an overarching, long-term strategy that provides a structure for the entire unit.

2. The O-T-Q strategy is more focused, short-term, and perhaps best as an introduction to an inquiry unit.

Both approaches involve elements that teachers have all used before, for example, tapping in to students' prior knowledge, getting them to ask a few questions, and reflecting on what they have learned. Teachers have all tried mightily to get students to be objective observers of what they see and hear and not jump to conclusions as they so often do, skipping the important steps of careful, precise observations verified with other observers.

Figure 5.1   Curricular Priorities/Orbitals

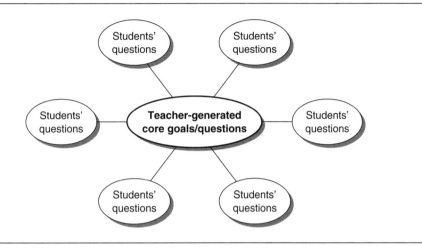

So what the teacher-student shared inquiry approach is proposing is not all that new, except that it suggests a major shift in who makes what kinds of decisions in the classroom. With this approach, students have more of a stake in their education—more sense of ownership in what's going on.

KWHLAQ

The major strategy is KWHLAQ. These letters represent the following questions (see Figure 5.2):

K   What do we think we **Know** about the subject?

W   What do we **Want/Need** to find out about it?

H   **How** will we go about finding out? How will we organize ourselves to investigate: use of time, access to resources, and planning for sharing findings?

L   What do we expect to **Learn**? What have we Learned?

A   How will we **Apply** what we have learned to other subjects? to our personal lives? to our next projects?

Q   What new **Questions** do we have following our inquiry?

By ending the inquiry with new questions, teachers fulfill several purposes:

- Teachers realize that new learnings can lead to more questions about new areas of knowledge not yet conceived
- Teachers round out the unit, beginning and ending with questions, thereby providing a neat curricular structure (this structure can then become internalized as teachers realize that one answer can lead to more questions)
- Teachers perpetuate student inquiry and make it more a part of their entire curriculum process

KWHLAQ

K What do we think we Know about the subject?

W What do we Want/Need to find out about it?

H How will we go about finding out? How will we organize ourselves to investigate: use of time, access to resources, and planning for sharing findings?

L What do we expect to Learn? What have we Learned?

A How will we Apply what we have learned to other subjects? to our personal lives? to our next projects?

Q What new Questions do we have following our inquiry?

Figure 5.2

Stop and Think

What do you think can be gained by challenging students to pose new questions at the end of a unit?

Advantages

The KWHLAQ has several advantages and some disadvantages. First, the KWHLAQ strategy taps into what students *think* they already know, thereby identifying prior knowledge and perhaps some misconceptions about important concepts. As we know from Marzano's (2003) research, accessing background knowledge is a significant step toward enhancing achievement.

Students get to ask some important questions of their own, thus reversing the usual control patterns in the classroom, so well documented over the years (Goodlad, 1984). Teachers do most of the talking and most of this is questioning that sometimes takes the form of a quiz show (Dillon, 1988).

This alteration of the usual patterns of domination by teachers is essential if teachers want students to buy into the content. Students must be given opportunities to identify what is important to them, to relate the subject matter to their own curiosities, their own puzzlements, their own gaps in knowledge. Without such opportunities to question freely and openly, classrooms remain teacher-dominated and therefore frustrating to many students. Teachers need to reflect on their own most meaningful learning experiences and determine how many of those experiences involved pursuing some area of personal interest in which they could make choices.

Teachers have an opportunity to help students analyze complex issues by asking, "What do we want and need to Know about this situation?" Research suggests that teachers in the United States focus more on students' achieving the right answer and less on their understanding the multiple ways to analyze a complex problem, especially in mathematics (Stevens & Stigler, 1992). Students' questions can become objectives for an entire unit, together with the teacher's central, core questions (see Figure 5.1). Students' questions, not just the teacher's, can lead the inquiry.

When we ask students, "What do we need to ask/determine about this situation?" we are treating them as young professionals in any subject. From this question we can generate class lists of the most important kinds of questions to ask related to the natural world, literature, historical events, number problems, art, health, and technological situations. Armed with these general questions, students are empowered to think and act more on their own.

This KWHLAQ strategy—by challenging students to figure out "How do we find answers?"—puts them in touch with multiple resources, such as the Internet, adults outside of school, and other students. It develops students' efficacy, ownership, and self-direction. As McCombs (1991) has noted, students need to recognize how our thinking patterns—beliefs about what we control and do not—determine our success and failures. "I can do this" versus "I'm never going to succeed" are significant self-talk messages we can control and, thereby, affect our success in life.

The attitude teachers work toward is, "I can control the thoughts that feed both positive and negative beliefs about how successful I can be" (McCombs, 1991, p. 9).

Toward this end, "Students need to have choice and support for autonomy" (McCombs, 1991, p. 10). Without the ability to make some choices within the instructional and curricular frameworks of the classroom, students will not experience the power of assuming some responsibility for their own learning. Many students, as judged by very informal surveys, realize that it is they who are responsible for getting a good education. What teachers must do is afford them opportunities to act responsibly to attain higher degrees of self-direction. A KWHLAQ strategy is one step toward this kind of empowerment.

Disadvantages

No matter how good any idea or strategy is, there are always some drawbacks.

Teachers will say, "It's hard work!" Yes, it is hard work and takes a real commitment to providing students with alternative means of becoming active participants in their own learning.

Teacher-student shared inquiry tends to be time consuming, because teachers spend more time planning, monitoring progress, and evaluating.

This inquiry process alters the teacher's role from disseminator of information (to use an old stereotype) to someone who guides students toward discovering some of their own answers. This requires more time structuring the process, helping to monitor progress, and prodding students to figure some things out for themselves (Barell, 2003; Perkins, 1992).

As students work on different questions/problems, more organizational skill, flexibility, and patience are required on the part of the teacher. Since students are used to being told what to do, some will at first balk at being on their own. Teachers must moderate their initiation by providing sufficient structure for those who need it. The amount of structure depends on age, the level of emotional and cognitive maturity, and the amount of experience in being away from the teacher's directions. The "boundaryless" characteristic of problematic scenarios (see Figure 4.2 in Chapter 4) will be discomforting for some teachers and students and that's why it's important to begin the change process incrementally. Some high achieving students will be too comfortable with previous learning patterns where they memorized great quantities of material to display on examinations. They will need time to deal with the unstructured, "boundaryless-ness" of PBL, but they will succeed.

Regardless of these disadvantages, teachers should seriously consider embarking on such an inquiry project if they are intrigued by the challenge to help students become more self-directed.

Stop and Think

 What are the advantages and disadvantages to implementing this type of inquiry in your own classroom?

Observe-Think-Question

The O-T-Q strategy is really a subdivision of the KWHLAQ strategy (see Figure 5.3). It commences not with "What do we know already?" but with "What do we observe?" Teachers can use it both as a variation or component of the KWHLAQ and when they want to help students become more sensitive to the need to get the facts first and then try to draw conclusions.

Observe: What do you notice about any specific object or situation? Make close observations, not inferences. Observations can be verified firsthand; they are what everyone can agree on. Inferences are conclusions based on data or evidence.

For example, a New York City resident observes that the weather during the month of January is unusually warm, fifty-five degrees Fahrenheit (temperatures are normally between 25 and 35 degrees Fahrenheit).

Think: Relate what you observe to what you already know about the subject. What similarities and differences do you notice between what you experience and what you have stored in memory? Are you noticing different aspects or elements? Did you recall experiences in a different way?

Following the example above, the resident realizes that this has happened before, but not every January. Sometimes the warm spell lasts a day or two, sometimes longer. The last warm spell coincided with the appearance of El Niño, the warming of Pacific Ocean currents that affects weather patterns in North America and other parts of the world.

Question: What curiosities arise from your investigations? What questions emerge from your comparisons between present or more recent experience and what you assumed to be true? Use these to propel the inquiry project.

To complete the example, the resident might logically ask if the warming spell in New York City is related to El Niño. What other causal factors might be operating, do these warm spells reflect global warming, and do they form a pattern over the years? These are questions definitely worth examining over the course of a unit on meteorology.

Too often, at all levels of schooling, teachers are chasing various assumptions and conclusions all around the classroom without having first agreed on the observable information. There are times when close attention to specific, concrete details must be first on the agenda. This naturally occurs in science classes where teachers ask, "What do we observe about this phenomenon?" These teachers are interested in students' becoming close observers of what they see.

For example, a teacher can ask a student who vacationed at Disney World, "While at Disney World what did you see, hear, feel, taste, and so forth?" This gives the student a whole database of information to reflect on. Then the teacher asks, "What did these observations make you think of?" The teacher wants the students to relate their observations to what they already know and

then hopes and expects that they might find some curiosities, some discontinuities, or some perplexing observations.

Advantages

As mentioned above several times, O-T-Q can be used easily as an introduction to helping students become good observers and questioners. We can use any artifact, picture, or experience to stimulate students' interest: quilts, poems, pictures of fossils, complex math situations.

O-T-Q provides opportunities to practice direct observations of factual information. It also helps highlight differences between facts and conclusions. This sounds very easy, but one teacher quickly discovered with a group of seventh graders examining two different kinds of plants that not only were students observing the color, shape, and smell of the leaves, stems, and root system, but they were also drawing conclusions, such as, "This plant seems to need water. This one is healthier. These leaves draw in more sunlight for photosynthesis." The teacher can pause here to give a short lesson on the difference between facts that can be verified objectively and judgments or claims that are drawn from these facts.

O-T-Q also allows teachers to spend time with close-in, detailed observations of what exists in other subjects, such as literature, history, fine and practical arts, foreign languages, and mathematics. Whenever teachers wish students to play the role of scientist, getting the facts straight first and then drawing conclusions, they need to take advantage of this kind of O-T-Q strategy. Again, this strategy elicits what students already know; therefore, it acts as a review of prior knowledge.

One major advantage of O-T-Q is that it places an emphasis on direct observation, one of the keys to fostering inquiry. Questions so often stem from direct, personal, and, if possible, objective observations of nature, of people, and human events. Too often we fail to pose good questions because we haven't taken the time to observe our surroundings. In all domains, in humanities and in math/science, we profit from becoming astute and keen observers of observable reality.

Disadvantages

One disadvantage is that students might initially not be very good at making firsthand observations. In that case, teachers can use students' lack of experience as a building block in their instructional program.

Another challenge is that we—students and teachers—often jump in with conclusions about a situation or an object without spending much time observing. We jump to conclusions, thereby getting lots of mental exercise, but we need others to say, "OK, what leads you to that tentative conclusion?"

Stop and Think

 What advantages and disadvantages do you see to using this format in your own classroom?

O-T-Q

Observe   What do you notice about any specific object or situation?

Think   Relate what you observe to what you already know about the subject.

Question   What curiosities arise from your investigations?

Figure 5.3

Other Strategies

Here are a few other strategies that can be used within the scope of the shared-inquiry approach.

Metacognitive Awareness

Teachers need to become more aware of their own thoughts and feelings so they can assume more control over them when they need to. Students and teachers ask themselves the following questions:

Plan: What is our question or problem and how will we work toward answers and solutions? (make a plan; set goals)

Monitor: How well is our inquiry proceeding? Do we need to change the question or goal? Seek alternative resources?

Evaluate: How well did we do? Did we reach our objective? Did we perform well? What might we do differently next time? Why? What did we learn about our thinking strategies? our feelings?

Modeling

Teachers need to model how they ask themselves questions and to encourage students to do the same. As mentioned above, a good way to begin is by starting a Thinking/Inquiry Journal for recording problems encountered and questions generated in everyday life.

Graphic Organizers

A good example of a graphic organizer for teacher-student shared inquiry is a concept map, similar to the one used throughout Chapter 4. Concept maps help teachers and students structure information in nonlinear ways (instead of a left-to-right sequence) to illustrate different points of view and multiple dimensions of a complex issue.

Small Group Inquiry/Research

Here students work toward answering teachers' and their own questions and might need instructions in how to proceed and monitor their own progress. At an early point in the school year students should identify the nature of good group work—"What does it look and sound like?"—and continually monitor their own progress toward this goal.

Whole Class Discussion: Critical Thinking

Class discussion need not be a mutual sharing of ideas or opinions without a focus. We should use such occasions for students to listen and learn from each other and to share different points of view, but usually with an objective of arriving at reasonable conclusions about an issue or solutions to a problem. These are good opportunities to practice critical thinking as defined by McPeck (1981) and Lipman (1988).

John McPeck: "Critical thought involves a certain skepticism, or suspension of assent, towards a given statement, established norm or mode of doing things."

Matthew Lipman: "Critical thinking is skillful, fully responsible thinking that facilitates judgments because it 1) relies upon criteria; 2) is self-correcting, and 3) is sensitive to context. . . . It is thinking that both employs criteria and that can be assessed by appeal to criteria."

We can ask students for their definitions, compare theirs with these scholars', and ask for preferences. Notice in McPeck's definition, critical thinking is defined as "a certain skepticism." This means asking necessary questions about a claim—"American cars will lose out to foreign made cars in ten years or less in terms of sales"—questions that have to do with sources, evidence, assumptions, definitions, and slant or bias. We can provide many opportunities for students to engage in this kind of critical thinking about editorials, commercials, pronouncements of quality and excellence from political leaders, and so forth (Barell, 2003).

And when students are given to say, "This is a terrible book!" we can challenge them with Lipman's demand for criteria when making a judgment, a claim, or drawing a conclusion. What makes a book (a class, a movie, TV show, game, political position or candidate) "terrible" or "terrific"? What are our judgment criteria or standards?

Use of Reflective Journals

Journals are good for note taking during investigations. They offer opportunities for students to raise questions continually as they proceed through their inquiry and to bring their questions to the attention of whole class.

Presentations/Reporting Results of Inquiry

Teachers can use these to culminate the unit with performances of understanding (Barell, 1995, 2003; Perkins, 1992).

Reflection

This is the last step in the metacognitive Plan, Monitor, and Evaluate process. Teachers and students need to think about how the process went and come up with ways to improve or continue on with the inquiry.

SAMPLE UNITS[1]

The following are three units, one each at the elementary, middle, and high school levels, that use these inquiry strategies. Again, these are composite portraits of three teachers who have had experience with these units in their own schools:

Beth/Middle School: Federal Government

David/High School: Where Is North America Going?

Susan/Elementary School: Emperor Penguins and Their Habitats

Sample Unit: Federal Government

Grade level: Middle School

Model: KWHLAQ

The sample units start with a unit Beth has undertaken with her middle school students. Beth is a teacher with several years' experience who wants to challenge her seventh and eighth graders to use their restless energies, both physical and mental, to explore issues and ideas more deeply than possible with the reading of one textbook. Beth likes the challenge of presenting students with opportunities to pose their own questions and problems. She feels her students can succeed because they have demonstrated abilities to act responsibly. Her students have worked in small groups, have kept journals in which they occasionally raise questions, and enjoy making presentations to the whole class. They love acting!

The KWHLAQ inquiry strategy lends itself to a simpler approach here. Beth wants to introduce her students to the major branches of government, their functions and roles in society, and challenge them to act like young legislators and executives creating and passing legislation and evaluating its constitutionality.

Before embarking upon this unit, Beth will have to map out all of the elements of the federal government she might conceivably deal with (see Paul's concept map, Figure 4.9 in Chapter 4), make choices among these elements in accordance with her state and subject matter standards, and, if possible, design a problematic scenario containing her major concepts and objectives.

As she maps out the major concepts, Beth is identifying for herself the major elements of this topic she needs students to think about and the broad areas into which her students' questions will most likely fall. This mapping process, therefore, is an excellent way to deal with lots of student questions as well as to include all state and subject matter standards she needs to consider.

Armed with this preparation, Beth can initiate her unit.

[What follows is a detailed and expanded version of how we can use the KWHLAQ with students. You will note that I have combined two processes: teacher planning before engaging students and what the teacher will do with students in class. As noted directly above, before ever asking, "What do we think we know?" Beth will have engaged in serious mapping, selecting, designing, and framing of the problems/questions and issues.]

What do we think we Know about the federal government?

Beth begins with a form of the O-T-Q approach by bringing in a variety of articles discussing various government issues. One concerns a controversial bill that some senators and representatives want to pass. She brings in one protecting the health of minors from the dangers of smoking and banning the sale of cigarettes within a mile of most elementary and middle schools with fines of up to $1,000 per incident for anyone caught and found guilty.

Students discuss the issue, and Beth finds that her students have strong feelings about the issues of freedom of choice and what the federal government can and cannot do. They disagree about whether such a bill could ever become law and about whether it violates any protections in the U.S. Constitution.

Now Beth has them hooked and can proceed with her first major question: What do we think we Know about the federal government, its components, and its powers? Beth organizes her students' responses on a concept map (see Figure 5.4).

Figure 5.4   Federal Government Concept Map I

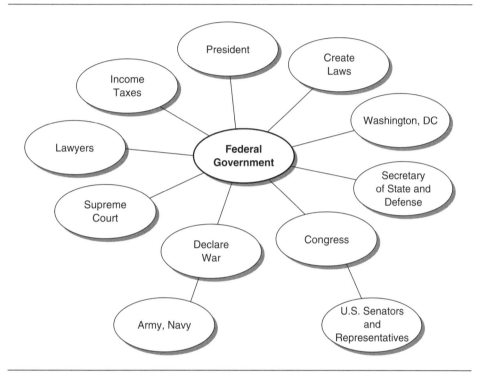

A science teacher may say, "I already know, after twenty years of teaching, what my students don't understand about electricity, so why should I ask this question?" There are so many good reasons for Beth to commence her unit of instruction with this question:

- She can acknowledge and value what her students already know, what they have learned from experience
- What they do know serves as a diagnostic foundation on which to build (Teachers are often pleasantly surprised to learn the extent of students' prior knowledge. One important teacher task is to help students relate new learnings to prior ones, and this question commences that process)
- She encounters students' misconceptions and false assumptions along the way

Stop and Think

Think of a unit of study in your own curriculum that would be useful in starting teacher-student shared inquiry. What type of question (or problem) would you pose to initiate the unit? Create a concept map for your own unit of study.

Beth inevitably encounters some errors of fact and misconceptions. Unless someone comments and corrects a prior comment, she honors each student's contribution, realizing that in the course of research, most of these errors or misjudgments will be corrected.

Another teacher may say, "My students are not used to this kind of question, and I have so many shy youngsters who won't participate!" The following are several things Beth does to encourage her students to participate:

- Starts with a concept map of something students do know (a pop or sports hero/heroine, favorite TV show, etc.); gives students the experience of her honoring what they already think they know
- When she makes the shift to the academic subject, she gives students some starters—"Think of people you've heard of, dates, places, objects, situations. . . . Think of similar situations. . . ." She might use a Think/Pair/Share to start here to encourage student participation
- Tries a Think/Pair/Share experience, in which students first do it on their own, then collaborate with a partner to add to their conceptual maps, and then share them with the large group

Beth keeps records of these initial gatherings of what students know. They can be used as she proceeds through the unit, adding on to students' information, and finally at the end of the unit she can compare what the students have learned with what they thought they knew just a few weeks ago by comparing concept maps (see Figure 5.5). Using different colored pencils each time she adds on to the map can help tell a story of how her students' knowledge developed over time (Allocco, personal communication, 1997).

Once the map is completed, Beth steps back and asks herself and her students, "Are there items on our map that can go together—that are related to each other?" One student sees that the word *Congress* is somehow related to the word *laws*. "Congress makes the laws," Judy says. Another student says the same thing about the Supreme Court and poses the first question, "Doesn't the Supreme Court do something with making laws illegal?" Already there are ambiguities in her students' minds.

Another student, Stephen, says, "Doesn't the president have something to do with laws also?" (another question). Then William sees a connection between the secretary of state and the president: "They work together don't they?" (a relationship and another question).

Here students in Beth's classroom are beginning to make connections and see relationships on their own. Then they can create categories of items:

- How laws are made
- The branches of government
- History
- What each branch does
- Problems

Identifying important characteristics and creating groups gives students good practice in classifying items, a skill that fosters intellectual development.

Beth can group her questions using any generalizations she and her students generate.

This reflection on what the students think they know affords Beth the opportunity to let students explore relationships. When students make connections among different ideas they are expanding their personal webs of meaningfulness. Every teacher knows this significant learning principle, but it bears reiterating here: *It is important for students to make connections, not only and always the teacher. Students learn from what* they *do, not from what teachers do for them* (Barell, 1995; Marzano, Pickering, & McTighe, 1992; Tyler, 1949).

What do we Want/Need to know about the federal government?

Teacher Planning. Beth needs to decide on some central problematic content questions/issues or problems for the unit as part of her unit planning. She wants to go into this kind of inquiry, at least in her early experiments with it, fully prepared with core issues. She needs to think through the concept of the federal government to identify what she thinks is most important for students to think productively about. For this, it's usually a good idea to create a concept map to picture all the significant elements as well as some of the relationships among them (see Figure 5.6).

Here are some central questions Beth might pose about any one of the three branches of the federal government:

- What are the roles and functions of each branch?
- What is the system of checks and balances? How does it work and why did the Founding Fathers create such a system?
- What changes have occurred within any branch since the adoption of the U.S. Constitution? For what reasons have these changes evolved?
- What is the role of any one branch in the following issues: civil rights, abortion, committing troops to a UN sponsored mission, balancing the federal budget?
- Analyze each branch for strengths and current weaknesses. What modifications to the U.S. Constitution would you recommend (e.g., amendments to balance the budget) and why?

These core questions become Beth's objectives. Just as in the previous teacher-directed unit (see Chapter 4), she needs the same clearly stated objectives. Beth's objectives come from her questions: Students will. . . .

- Describe the role and function of different branches of government
- Explain checks and balances and analyze situations where they are applicable
- Examine changes to the U.S. Constitution and in the amendments and give reasons for and against specific amendments in the past (e.g., Prohibition, presidential term limits) and proposed amendments that would ban flag burning and gay marriage

Figure 5.5 First Map/Second Map/Concluding Map

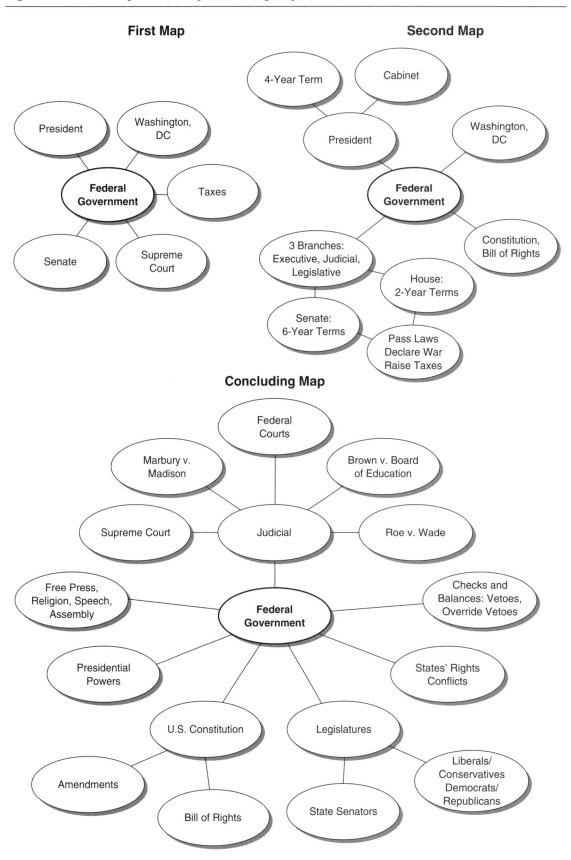

Figure 5.6   Federal Government Concept Map II

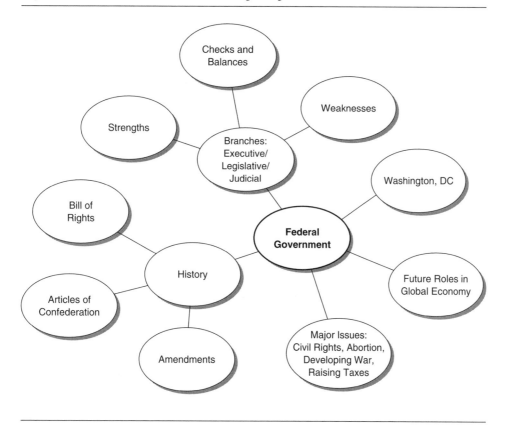

- Analyze situations where the federal government can play a role (e.g., abortion, equal rights, deployment of U.S. troops) and determine what that role is and recommend any future changes
- Redesign the U.S. Constitution for the middle of the twenty-first century and give good reasons for their choices

To these objectives Beth adds the students' areas of interest and concern. Their questions become additional objectives for the unit.

The core questions should meet all the criteria regarding problematic situations: complexity, interesting to students and teachers, robust within the subject matter, foster inquiry (fascinating), elements transferable to other subjects/personal lives, and significant socially/culturally (see Chapter 4 for a more in-depth explanation of criteria regarding problematic situations).

Why does Beth want to have central, core issues while engaged in the KWHLAQ kind of inquiry strategy? The following are several reasons:

- Provides her with some control over outcomes
- Helps her organize the unit around core concepts that she must deal with as part of the curriculum
- Provides an organizational focus for all student questions

An alternative to identifying these core issues beforehand is for Beth and her students to develop the core questions collaboratively. This requires more

flexibility on Beth's part, as well as more maturity and experience from her students.

Developing core questions and objectives with students is a step Beth can take if she is undertaking a unit with more leeway—where she has more flexibility. With the federal government she has the perennial issue of "covering content" and the need to be mindful that students can think productively about checks and balances, for example, as well as about questions such as, "Was Ronald Reagan [or any other president] a good president?"

Beth realizes that middle school students might not really want to know too much about what goes on in Washington, DC, so she frames a small problem for them, "Suppose you are a reporter for our school newspaper and you are covering the story about smoking/flag burning/gay marriage that we started with. What would you *need* to know about the federal government to write an accurate and convincing story?" By personalizing this phase of the inquiry, Beth may receive more input.

Students' Questions. Beth lists questions students pose after they look over all of their prior knowledge, assumptions, and perhaps some misconceptions. Some of these questions come forth as students identify what they think they know:

- Who makes the laws of the country?
- Doesn't the Supreme Court have something to do with making laws illegal?
- What does the president really do, besides fly around in a helicopter, give speeches, and be in meetings all day?
- Can a U.S. senator be born in another country?
- Who was John F. Kennedy?
- Can a state ever tell the government in Washington what to do?
- How long have we had a government in Washington?
- Can the president go to war?
- What was *Brown v. Board of Education*?
- Why do we have to have two houses in Congress?
- Was Ronald Reagan a good president?

These are initial questions to start the unit. As Beth gathers more information and ideas, new questions arise.

Stop and Think

 How do we help students organize these questions and plan their use of time, access to resources and sharing of findings?

Here are some initial steps for students to help identify core unit objectives:

- Students identify questions of interest
- Students group themselves around common questions

- Students identify resources—when and where they are available
- Teachers introduce students to the metacognitive strategy of Planning, Monitoring, and Evaluating

What Beth has now are students' questions that supplement her own core objectives—what absolutely must be dealt with in the unit. These student questions can be visualized as orbiting around the teacher's central questions, sort of like the planets of our solar system (see Tomlinson, 1999, p. 71, for description of "orbitals"; see also Figure 5.1 in this chapter).

Sometimes we spend far too little time in schools challenging students to analyze situations (Goodlad, 1984; Stevens & Stigler, 1992). Too often, students are passive recipients of information. Students need to take some responsibility and try to figure out a complex situation, such as they were presented with in Beth's initiating activity—a bill proposed to ban the sale of cigarettes near schools. Raising critical questions (see McPeck's definition of critical thinking, above) helps students become more analytical in their thinking. It should also promote their thinking as if they were professionals out in the field encountering a complex situation requiring analysis and investigation.

Kinds of Questions

Beth can use the Three-Story Intellect (see Figure 2.3), which differentiates between gathering, processing, and applying questions, to model different levels of questions. For example, referring to the list of questions Beth's students posed, Beth asks students, "What differences do you see between these two questions: 'Who was John F. Kennedy?' and 'Was Ronald Reagan a good president?'" She discusses with students what they are asking someone to do when they ask each question. The first question asks one to identify who a person was. This involves either remembering that John F. Kennedy was the president of the United States or looking it up. In the second question students would probably say, "You have to give your opinion." Looking at the Three-Story Intellect model Beth can see that her students are operating on two different levels: gathering and applying. In the last question, students are evaluating one man's performance on the job and this means developing criteria for a "good president," a very complex task. See Matt Lipman's definition of critical thinking, above. (Note: Depending on the intellectual sophistication of students, some might see the first question as one calling for character analysis as well.)

Using these examples, Beth can use other questions from the students' list or illustrate different questions with personal examples. When students ask, "What goes together? What are we doing?" they are using the second level, classifying. When students ask, "Why did the president go to war against Iraq in Desert Storm (1991) and in Operation Iraqi Freedom (2003)?" they are asking someone to analyze and give good reasons.

Beth can also start students off with question stems that elicit good questions. She can ask students to start with who, what, when, where, why, and how questions or questions that ask others to remember, to compare, to find reasons, to create hypothetical (What if . . . ?) situations, and to evaluate.

Another option is for Beth to teach the concept of flexibility and, using a graphic (e.g., a concept map), to help students think of how to approach a situation or topic from different points of view (see Figure 5.7).

Figure 5.7   Achieving Flexibility in Perspective

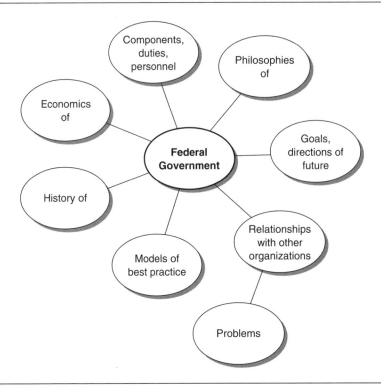

When Beth poses questions from different points of view she has a more flexible approach to a situation, compared with generating questions that are all, for example, about history or about essential components. This is different from merely generating long lists of questions that all deal with the same aspect of the situation, say history. According to Perkins (1992), when teachers speak of problem solving, flexibility is more important for generating creative solutions than fluency (the number of ideas or questions).

Beth could even have students keep journals. Then her students can use their journals as sources of continuing questions during the ongoing inquiry.

Once Beth has received good questions from her students, she can work with students to identify patterns/relationships among the questions. "Which questions seem similar to you? Which go together and why?" Here is a good opportunity to explore connections. The more connections Beth can identify and establish, the more focused and meaningful students' research will be.

Once students have a set of questions worthy of spending some time on, they have their own problematic situations. In the previous teacher-directed unit (see Chapter 4), teachers identified the complex phenomenon worth investigating with a problematic scenario ("You are. . . ."). Now the balance of control is shifted somewhat to tell students that their questions represent problems to them, curiosities that stimulate their own inquiry.

Teacher-Directed PBL	Teacher-Student Shared Inquiry
Teacher creates "You are. . . ." Scenario	Students' questions = problems (And, of course, we can add a "You are. . . ." problematic)

Again, it is important for Beth to encourage students to take more responsibility for their own learning by engaging in setting criteria as well as working to classify and analyze their own questions. Students will be looking for comparisons and underlying assumptions, and projecting possible outcomes. Teachers should ask them, "If we work on this question, what kinds of information will we get? Do we want to know this? How will these questions help us?"

Beth considers the following criteria for students' selection of their questions:

- Meaningful/fascinating to students
- Important to the subject and state standards
- Represent Levels II or III of the Three-Story Intellect (see Figure 2.3)
- Relates to the core question
- Lots of students posed it (and/or voted for its inclusion)
- Resources are available
- Beth and her students consider it novel and fascinating
- Encourages students to explore a new area

Stop and Think

Think about the unit of study you decided to use for teacher-student shared inquiry. What kinds of questions/curiosities/problematic situations are students going to investigate? List your own criteria. (This would be a good experience for students, identifying why they select questions to inquire about. What makes them important?)

How will we go about finding the answers to these questions?

In posing this question, Beth asks students to figure out how to find their own answers and how to organize the classroom for serious investigation. The first involves access to resources; the latter involves classroom management.

Chances are they haven't had much experience in responding to this kind of question, just as they haven't spent too much time in classrooms posing their own questions. But Beth finds that they have lots of ideas:

- People (adults in and out of school, students in other schools reached through e-mail, parents/grandparents, etc.)
- Electronic resources (Internet, e-mail, CD-ROMs)
- Print media (books, magazines)
- Film (video- and audiotapes, films)
- Public media (TV, radio)
- Dramatic media (theaters)
- Museums
- Exhibitions
- Conferences
- Themselves! (Students usually think of what they already know last!)

They are not used to seeing themselves and classmates as resources. Very often as students are asking questions, one of their classmates will have an answer. Students seem a lot more comfortable answering questions than posing them and that certainly is understandable. That's what their lives in a classroom have been like.

How do we organize ourselves for investigations?

The second charge is to help students organize their investigations. Obviously, this will take different pathways depending upon age and grade level. I have seen fourth graders follow the KWHLAQ format with much needed structuring from their teacher and with the teacher making most management decisions while students were researching their own questions during a unit on rocks. (Ann White, East Orange, NJ)

I have seen a ninth-grade teacher (Cheryl Hopper, Paramus, NJ) during a unit on Africa basically leave it up to her students—average in ability by her account—to figure out resources, make lesson plans complete with homework assignments for the unit (plans that always included a role for her, by the way), and even lead tours at a local museum exhibiting African art.

What will be helpful here is our Planning, Monitoring, and Evaluating triad of self-management questions.

Plan: What is our task? How will we manage time, access to resources, collaborative sharing of findings, and prepare for culminating projects and feedback?

Perhaps weekly we should monitor our progress:

Monitor: How well are we doing? Do we have new questions to answer? Do we need different resources?

At unit's end we should assess what we've learned and accomplished:

Evaluate: How well did we do? Did we answer our question(s)? What might we do differently next time? Why?

Again, we can challenge students of different ages to share in the ownership of unit planning to varying degrees.

It's important to encourage students' acceptance of ever-increasing degrees of responsibility as they grow through their school years. The goal is to teach them that they are not in school to follow orders but to figure out how to accomplish increasingly complex tasks using their own resources and their own thinking. Even if they perceive barriers, students can override these negative thoughts "by an understanding that I can control the thoughts (and, hence, the emotions) that feed those beliefs. *I can choose to redirect my thoughts*" (McCombs, 1991, p. 9; emphasis added) and hence my actions toward more fruitful goals.

Critical Analysis of Situations: Comparing/Contrasting

During this all-important phase while students are organizing their investigations and gathering information, teachers can be engaged in helping students sift through the amazing amounts of information they will acquire.

Beth may want to use McPeck's definition of critical thinking as "a certain skepticism" to foster their asking good questions about reliability of sources and evidence, underlying assumptions and definitions, and slant or bias in the information they are finding on the Web or in books.

Another important critical thinking skill, demonstrated by Marzano, Pickering, and Pollock (2001) to directly and positively affect student achievement, is comparing and contrasting. Why is this such an important intellectual skill? Perhaps because it involves identifying key attributes, distinguishing those from others that are unimportant for our purposes, creating classifications, and ordering items into categories from concrete to more abstract. These processes are significant because they help us make sense of our complex world experiences. For example, they are the basis for creating metaphors in poetry and drama (as well as for designing models in science; e.g., the brain as a computer). "Presenting students with explicit guidance in identifying similarities and differences enhances students' understanding of and ability to use knowledge" (p. 15).

As students gather information during the core learning experiences, they not only reflect on it, they analyze it. This means they determine what is important in the questions they have posed and suggests that they engage in critical analysis using a set of criteria for what they consider vital. They also seek to relate disparate pieces of information, looking for those hidden likenesses or connections that Bronowski (1965, 1978) thought were the basis for creativity in the arts and sciences.

This sounds quite easy to do, but structuring learning experiences to help students seek out connections among a lot of disparate information is not always achieved.

To help students seek connections, Beth must realize that students often make connections directly between two events, subjects, or concepts that seem similar. For example, there are connections between two different major league baseball teams, two different presidents, and the concept of freedom is present in two different struggles of minorities in the United States.

However, very often the mark of an intelligent person is the ability to make connections where they are not so evident, where they are not a matter of superficial similarities. For these deeper relationships Beth's students must become more adept at identifying the underlying connections. How do they do this? One way might be to become more adept at identifying the essential characteristics of events, subjects, or concepts.

For example, students may read about the *Brown v. Board of Education* case in their research on the judicial branch of the federal government, and they might encounter the Civil Rights Act of 1964. Here are actions by two separate branches of government. What do they have in common? One way to find out is with Venn diagrams (see Figures 5.8 and 5.9).

If Beth helps her students identify the essential characteristics of each, they will, of course, find that both are actions of the federal government concerned

Figure 5.8   Beth's Venn Diagram

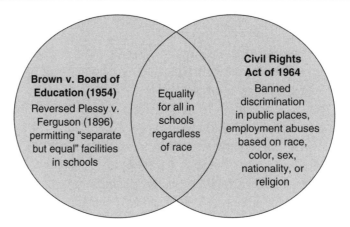

with equal rights of all people in the country, one having to do solely with schooling and the other having to do with freedoms in such areas as voting, employment, and housing.

Giving students examples or, better yet, using examples from their own research provides ample, as well as authentic, opportunities to identify significant characteristics and begin to find the connections between events, subjects, or concepts. This ability is developmentally driven. Younger students are guided more by surface, external characteristics, whereas older students, those in middle and high schools, are better able to look beyond or beneath the surface to find the "hidden likenesses" that might reveal more subtle or conceptual similarities and relationships (see Figure 5.10).

Beth can encourage her students to seek connections by having students write in their journals about the connections they are finding, and by checking the journals periodically to monitor students' progress. Beth can display and share with the class the connections students are finding as they conduct their research and then ask other students to identify the relationships. Beth needs to discuss the value of these relationships for the questions under discussion and analyze the quality of the relationships. Just because one person sees a connection doesn't mean that everyone does, or that everyone agrees that it is germane to the issues at hand.

Stop and Think

What steps can you take in your own units of study to help students become better at finding those "hidden likenesses" Bronowski wrote about?

What are we Learning and what have we Learned about the federal government?

One thing I've learned from good teachers is that they assess the learning of their students daily and weekly. This phase of the process is therefore not confined to the end of a unit. Rather we are continually asking, "What are we learning? What new questions do we have?"

VENN DIAGRAM

Compare and Contrast These Two Phenomena

Question:

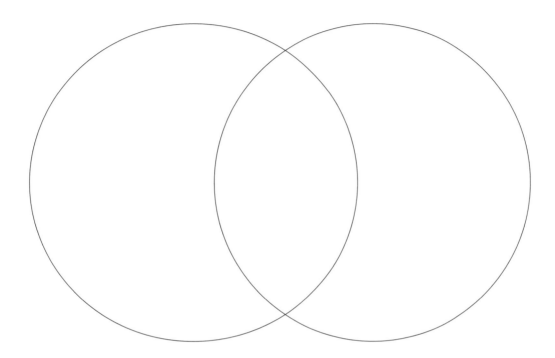

Draw Your Own Conclusions:

Too often we compare/contrast without completing the process by drawing our own conclusions. What can we reasonably conclude, following our analysis?

_____

_____

_____

_____

_____

_____

_____

_____

_____

_____

Figure 5.9

SEEKING AND FINDING HIDDEN LIKENESSES/CONNECTIONS

For practice in finding connections and establishing relationships, give students examples of seemingly disparate events, subjects, or concepts. Have them map out essential characteristics, compare and contrast, and then draw conclusions about their similarities and differences.

Events/Subjects and Essential Characteristics

Great Society Legislation: Federal money for housing, education, and equal employment opportunities, primarily for the poor

Roe vs. Wade: Federal legislation granting women the right to have an abortion up to a certain time after conception

Bill of Rights: The first ten amendments to the U.S. Constitution granting freedoms, such as speech, religion, right to bear arms, and assembly

The Bay of Pigs: A failed military assault on Cuba during the first months of the Kennedy administration that attempted to liberate Cuba from the communism of Castro

Perceived Connections

All these acts involve all three branches of the federal government—executive, judicial, and legislative—and had to do with the rights of certain people to freedoms, to equal access to employment, to speak their minds, to control their bodies, and to live under a different form of government. Another way to look at these is that they are examples of the federal government's exercising its powers in areas that some feel it should not do so (namely, *Roe vs. Wade,* The Bay of Pigs, and the Great Society Legislation).

Figure 5.10

Before presenting research results at unit's end, Beth must ensure that her students have spent sufficient time drawing their own conclusions. This is a critical step, because Beth does not want to see, hear, or listen to a repetition of lots of encyclopedic information undistilled by students' own thinking. This is critical thinking at its most important. Lipman (1988) has defined critical thinking as the making of judgments in accordance with criteria, a process that is self-correcting and sensitive to context.

One way for Beth to help her students draw their own conclusions is to define a conclusion. There are a number of possible definitions: to bring to a close or to end, to bring to a settlement or decision, to determine by reasoning, or to infer. When Beth brings the investigation to an end, the conclusion can be seen as an answer to the original (or modified) question. For example, with the original question, "Was Ronald Regan a good president?" students might decide yes or no and give their reasons using Lipman's definition of critical thinking as making a judgment in accordance with criteria. ("What makes a 'good' leader?"; e.g., ability to communicate with the public about visions, problems; decisive decision maker; able to identify key issues and muster support of populace; curious about the world and life; reflective; etc.)

Another way Beth can help students draw conclusions is to return to her and her students' initial questions to refresh their memories about the nature of their inquiry. What were they trying to find out? If one of the questions was, "Should judges be elected?" then their conclusions would answer this question and give reasons, reasons that take into account arguments both pro and con and why they chose the alternative they did. Here is where critical thinking becomes very evident. Students must ask, "What are the reasons why we have drawn our conclusions? What kinds of evidence have we marshaled to convince ourselves and perhaps others?" and, just as important, "What evidence contradicts our conclusion? What are other points of view?"

Beth can assess the quality of the conclusions using the following criteria:

Reasonable: Does it derive from sufficient information and evidence to support the conclusion? (For example, can students conclude that they need a balanced budget amendment to the U.S. Constitution from the fact that for so many years the federal budget has been out of balance? Can they conclude that they need a special cabinet position on Women's Rights due to the fact that women in the workforce often are paid less than their male counterparts?) Ensure that students present sufficient reasons supported by factual information to the extent possible.

Practical: Can it work, given the structures of government and the nature of society?

Significant: Are the conclusions meaningful, do they make an important contribution? For example, are recommendations for congressional term limits important?

Stop and Think

How do you help students draw their own conclusions? Jot down conclusions about a unit you have just completed, ones you perceive students reaching, and assess them in accordance with your own criteria.

Well before students are ready with their conclusions, Beth must introduce them to the concepts of alternative, authentic, and performance assessments (these three different aspects of assessment are discussed in detail in Chapter 8).

Alternative assessments reflect the many and varied ways we all have of expressing ourselves and sharing meanings:

- Written reports and projects
- Aesthetic products of all kinds: poetry, drama, drawing/painting/film
- Creating models; metaphors and analogies
- PowerPoint presentations before experts
- Debates, interviews, panel discussions, and the like

Authentic describes assessments that reflect what occurs in life beyond the classroom using those intellectual processes in Levels II and III and what Newmann called "cognitive work found in the adult world." If Beth is asking students to understand the concept of balance of powers, an authentic assessment would engage them in analyzing actual legislative situations where this concept is found (e.g., perhaps in the papers, on news telecasts). They could play the role of news analysts or editorial writers. She could also challenge them to apply this principle of balance of powers to the British Parliamentary system and to create a Utopia where this principle found a different manifestation.

Performance means students are engaged in a demonstration of their understanding of knowledge and skills (Barell 1995, 2003; Perkins 1992; Wiggins 1993). For example, students could deliver their conclusions as TV commentators.

This is the culminating learning experience, with emphasis on the word *learning*. Assessments should not be recitations of what Beth and her students already know. Assessments should be opportunities for students to assimilate all their ideas into conclusions that they can explain and answer questions about. "Assessment of thoughtful mastery should ask students to justify their understanding and craft, not merely to recite orthodox views or mindlessly employ techniques in a vacuum" (Wiggins, 1993, p. 47).

Stop and Think

How would you assess students' understanding of the kinds of questions posed in one of your own units?

Once students have completed their presentations, they are ready for a final evaluative, metacognitive reflection on their own thinking and learning. A good way to engage students in reflection is through journal writing. They can respond to these kinds of questions:

- What learnings have been most important to me? Why?
- What have I learned about my thinking? my feelings?
- How do I feel about myself as a questioner? a researcher? a group member?
- What do I want to get better at? (new strategy or goal setting)

How will we Apply what we have learned about the federal government to other subjects?

Making the transfer connection is a continuation of the metacognitive strategy and emphasizes continuity and integration within other curricular units (Tyler, 1949). Beth asks, "How can we apply new learnings to other subjects?"

Teachers don't always pose the application question. Too often, they are content with their students' being able to define relevant vocabulary or to answer questions asked at the beginning of the unit. The next to the last step of the KWHLAQ strategy—what Tyler (1949) called integration of knowledge across subject matter lines—the application to other areas within the same subject or in other subjects, is not pressed.

Stop and Think

 Take the concepts or ideas learned in this unit about the federal government, or ideas from your own unit of study, and see how they relate to other subjects or to your students' lives beyond school.

These are some of the ways Beth thinks she can help her students transfer their learnings:

Learnings	Related to Other Subjects/Life Beyond School
Checks and balances Keep three branches working harmoniously, preventing one from becoming "imperial" "We, the people . . ." are empowered to control our own destiny as a nation	Balancing check books, equations, etc. Cooperation within any community of government scholars, such as scientists Personal control within life situations

What new Questions do we have about the federal government following our inquiry?

This completes the inquiry cycle. As noted earlier, ending the unit with reflection and application calls for Beth to bring the unit full circle to the new

curiosities raised by what her students have learned. Students can now generate new questions that might lead to the next unit, to independent study, or to their own personal pursuits. Beth can generalize these questions so they have more applicability in all her studies. For example, she might help students realize that if they ask certain kinds of questions as per McPeck's definition of critical thinking ("a certain skepticism"), they will become more informed. Questions about information can be very helpful:

- What is the source?
- What is the evidence and is it believable? reliable?
- What are the assumptions underlying this situation?
- Are there words/concepts we need to define?
- Can we identify any slant or bias in the reporting? Any favored special interests among the parties to the situation?

Questions like these help Beth and her students become better critical inquirers (Barell, 2003).

Everyone needs to be reflective. When students have completed their inquiry and Beth has helped them work through the KWHLAQ process, she should reflect on her own performance to determine what she has learned about herself, her teaching, and her relationship with students. Beth asks herself the following questions:

- What did I learn about myself as teacher? my students? the subject?
- What elements of this unit can I use in other units?
- How can what I did be beneficial to other teachers?
- How would I share such learnings?

Beth engages in these reflections just as her students do, as part of her own Plan, Monitor, and Evaluate process; alone or with colleagues; in words; and perhaps in journals.

What she can do to impress on students the importance of this process is to share her thoughts and reflections with students. When she is asking them to reflect on their own learnings she can add her own reflections, thereby acting as a good model.

Sample Unit: Where Is North America Going?

Grade level: High School

Model: O-T-Q

In the following sample unit, David uses something called a strange phenomenon, what cognitive psychologists might call a discrepant event, as a starting point. Such an event or experience is one that presents challenges to the normal way of looking at things. It challenges preconceived assumptions and gets students to ask questions.

In the sciences these events present contradictions to prior understandings:

- Evidence of dinosaur bones deep in Antarctica
- Behavior of a bimetallic strip over a Bunsen burner

- A glass full over the top with water that doesn't spill
- The Venus flytrap plant closes on insects after exactly two hits on one leaf hair or one hit on two hairs simultaneously

For this unit David wants to focus on the history of the Earth, how it has developed, what the Earth's crust consists of, how scientists determine geological ages, fossils, and what forces have affected the movement of continents across the surface. This is his content.

He wants to engage students in the inquiry process; therefore, he expects them to generate a lot of questions that they can pursue in small groups as they think productively about the concepts outlined in his content.

For objectives David expects his average non–college-bound students to be able to do the following:

1. Know and describe the various elements of the Earth's composition (the basic ages through which it has passed)

2. Describe plate tectonics

3. Apply this knowledge to current and appropriate geological problems

4. Construct their own models of geological forces

His initiating strategy is the O-T-Q. For this he needs a fascinating illustration that depicts the effects of plate tectonics. Figure 5.11 illustrates what geologists like Ian Dalziel (1995) think are the most reasonable conclusions about what Earth's surface looked like over the past 1 billion years. He uses as evidence rock formations in North America, Antarctica, and Europe. Dalziel has also used another significant source of information—magnetization of iron-bearing rock that indicates its longitudinal alignment when it cooled from the molten state.

Thus, Figure 5.11 reflects not direct evidence (e.g., from the rocks and their magnetic orientations), but reasoned conclusions (inferences) that support Alfred Wegener's theory of continental drift, suggesting that the continents have moved from other positions on Earth to where they are now. So when David challenges his students to Observe the images, they are looking at one geologist's hypothesis—drawn from years of examining the evidence—about how continents have moved and merged over the past several hundred million years.

For a current representation of plate tectonics and their effects on Earth's continents' movements, visit the U.S. Geological Survey's "Historical perspective" page at http://pubs.usgs.gov/gip/dynamic/historical.html.

David wants his students to compare these pictures with the known configurations of the planet's surface, so having a globe on hand is important.

Observe

David asks his students what they observe: "What do you notice about these drawings? What seems interesting or different to you?" David then posts all observations on the board and notes students' names alongside to acknowledge their contributions. These are some of the responses David received:

1. The continents are in different places.
2. They don't stay in one place over time.

Figure 5.11 Plate Tectonics

Neoproterozoic
(750 Million Years Ago)

Latest Neoproterozoic
(550 Million Years Ago)

Middle Cambrian
(530 Million Years Ago)

Mid-Ordovician
(487 Million Years Ago)

Mid-Silurian
(422 Million Years Ago)

Lare Devonian
(374 Million Years Ago)

Early Permian
(260 Million Years Ago)

Northern Europe

South America

Australia, Antarctica, and India

Africa

North America

Siberia

SOURCE: Ian Worpole for *Scientific American.*

3. Something's pushing them around. (An observation or an inference?)

4. They seem to be next to different places at different times.

5. Nothing stays still. (Observation or inference?)

6. The continents are different colors. (One student might respond, "That's the way they do it for the book!")

7. North America has moved around a lot; it seems to move from South to North here.

8. Locations of the oceans change.

9. Are we looking at the same side of the Earth in all these pictures? (The first inquiry.)

10. Africa seems to rotate in all those millions of years.

Now David asks his students, "Are any of these observations similar? Can we tie any of them together?" Students might, for example, say that they all have to do with movement of the continents. Then someone might observe that two observations (numbers 7 and 10) indicate a certain direction of motion (rotation) and perhaps others do as well. Another classification might be created with reference to the size of the oceans (number 8).

His students create different classifications, which gives him an idea of the scope of the challenge the students will face in trying to make connections and subsume particular observations under more general categories.

Think

David has students relate the information to what they already know about earth history, its systems and basic principles of geology. He tells his students to ask themselves, "What do these observations make me think of?" The students identify their prior learnings, understandings, assumptions, and beliefs. They may have lots of ideas stored up from prior experience or only sketchy impressions, but if David can tap into these he might be able to identify some of those perplexities that foster inquiry and thinking. Here he is reinforcing or approaching the K of the KWHLAQ from a different point of view. Students might tap into the following kinds of background knowledge:

- Rock types and formations
- Age of the Earth
- Oceans, coverage of the Earth
- Plate tectonics
- Wegener's theory of continental drift
- Earth's magnetic structure
- Different kinds of plate movements—convergent, divergent, and transform boundaries

Here is where David wants students to match what they know with what they are observing to see if there are any puzzling situations that arise.

Question

Now David asks his students to question what they observe against the background of what they think they know. He begins to get questions as he makes observations (number 9 under Observe).

David asks:

- What strikes you as curious about your observations?
- What doesn't make sense?
- What would puzzle a geologist looking at these pictures?

Students reply:

- Are the continents really moving?
- Why do the continents move?
- How did they form and separate?
- Do they always move? at the same speed?
- Are they moving now?
- Are earthquakes related to these changes we see?
- What will happen in the next 100 million years?
- Can we stop these movements? (a few laughs from other students)
- What keeps them moving, if we can't stop them?
- Do all continents move? Did they?
- Where is North America going?

Then David works with students to organize their questions for inquiry.

Stop and Think

 How would you organize the class's inquiry from here on? What steps do you think would be essential?

Now that David and his students have used the O-T-Q process to negotiate a problem, they can engage in the inquiry process:

1. Organize the questions; look for similarities, possible categories

2. Find the central, core question; for example, "How do geologists analyze and understand the Earth's geological formations and how they came to their present configurations?" (or, "You are a USC geologist given the charge to predict one continent's movements over the next 100 million years. How would you go about doing this? See if you can confirm or disconfirm Dalziel's hypothesis en route to your conclusions.")

3. Conduct research (core experience)

4. Analyze and relate findings

5. Report (culminating experience)

6. Assess progress (show some small graphics)

7. Reflect

8. Apply and transfer

9. Create new questions

David can proceed with a full KWHLAQ from here, engaging students in organizing their investigations. When he asks how they would find answers to their questions, they will obviously mention using the Internet as one source, together with speaking with local experts—geologists and geophysicists—who will help them understand what they have observed. Together teacher and students can organize class time to access resources, share and think critically about findings, and prepare final projects and culminating assessments.

During their investigations, David will introduce key geological concepts and asking critical questions about data and evidence gleaned from a wide variety of sources.

Assessments within this unit can be developed together with students: "How will you be able to demonstrate to me that you know and understand the geologic forces at work in Dalziel's picture?" Students will generate a variety of alternative assessment experiences such as creating projects, models, making videos, and writing stories and analytic reports.

At some point David will ask, "How will we assess your presentation for the quality of understanding?" Students will probably identify criteria such as Organization, Presentational Skills, Knowledge, and Understanding of Geology. Teachers might want to add to this list Quality of Scientific Reasoning (e.g., asking good questions, assessing data for reliability/accuracy/sample size, and ability to draw reasonable conclusions). See Chapter 8 for more on assessing David's unit.

Sample Unit: Emperor Penguins and their Habitats

Grade level: Elementary School

Model: KWHLAQ

Children of all ages love penguins. Whenever children see them, penguins bring a smile to their faces. They walk funny, dress like people off to a formal ball, and toboggan across the ice on their white bellies propelled by two powerful flippers that perhaps once were wings. They are an endless source of delight and an excellent focus for an animal biology unit at any grade level.

Susan knows her fourth graders love animals. They have studied dinosaurs as well as animals from the rain forest. Now she really wants to engage them in generating their own questions about animals that are very different from ones they have studied before, ones that inhabit the southern-most continent, Antarctica. So Susan starts with their habitat.

In this unit, Susan also integrates several perspectives simultaneously. Therefore, she is interested not only in the science of these polar creatures but also in the history and literature of the region as told by various explorers, from Scott and Shackleton to Amundsen and Byrd. She may also include some mathematical calculations related to scientific investigations.

Figure 5.12 Concept Map of Antarctica

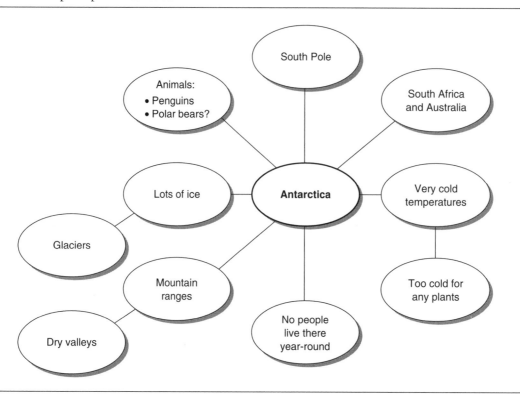

What do we think we Know about Antarctica?

As a way of introducing this unit and capturing her students' imaginations, Susan shows a number of video clips of Antarctica, perhaps including portions of the Oscar-winning documentary *March of the Penguins*. Students will marvel at the amazing story of how and when Emperor penguins breed and survive harsh Antarctic winters.

After students become excited about this very strange, forbidding continent with its equally perplexing yet beautiful animal life, she can ask, "What do we think we know about this continent?"

Susan receives a lot of misinformation and many misconceptions about this frozen continent. For example, there is confusion about the kinds of animals that live there (polar bears?), whether there is land or is it just ice (as at the North Pole?), and so forth. As with all inquiry projects, Susan accepts all the answers unless someone can say definitely that polar bears live only up north (True). She compiles all the student responses in a concept map (see Figure 5.12).

What do we Want/Need to know about Antarctica?

Susan can ask her students, "If you are a young animal biologist investigating life in very challenging environments like Antarctica, what do you need to know?" Here Susan can couple her inquiry with the You are. . . . strategy introduced with teacher-directed investigations (see Chapter 4). As we've mentioned on several occasions, here is where we can introduce students to beginning to think like professionals, in this case like young scientists. We hope over time—during their lives in school—that they will use challenges like this to begin to identify the foundational questions all good professionals ask when beginning their investigations. One of our goals in education is to provide students with sufficient experiences wherein they can play the role of young experts learning the kinds of questions we need to ask in order to understand a situation. In Susan's case, such questions might have to do with animal characteristics ("What does it do?"), about mating practices, about how it survives within its environment, about relationships with other creatures (e.g., predators), and what happens if the environment changes.

Stop and Think

 What kinds of questions would you pose about one of nature's most curious characters?

Susan decides to focus on Emperor penguins in the Antarctica. Here are a few questions she and her students pose:

- How do they survive?
- Who are their natural predators?
- How long do they live?
- Why do they always seem to travel in large groups?
- Do all penguins mate in the same way?
- Do they have lifelong mates?
- How are they different from the Adélie penguins?
- Did they once fly?
- Are they related to the dinosaurs?
- How do they survive swimming in such cold waters?

Susan encourages some questions about the penguins' future, given her class's previous study of the suspected ecological effects of burning fossil fuels (e.g., global warming, ozone depletion). She wants her students to pose the question and work as scientists who can generate some positive proposals for change.

How will we go about finding answers to our questions?

Here Susan wants her students to create their own lists of resources. Many students will have seen *March of the Penguins*, and they may know of the Discovery Channel's excellent videos, including *Planet of Ice*. Of course students will find valuable information on the Internet at various Web sites about Antarctic scientific stations like

McMurdo: http://astro.uchicago.edu/cara/vtour/mcmurdo/

South Pole: http://astro.uchicago.edu/cara/vtour/pole/

Mawson (Australian): http://www.aad.gov.au/asset/webcams/mawson/default.asp

Vostok (Russian): http://www.antarcticconnection.com/antarctic/stations/vostok.shtml

They can hear Emperor penguins sneeze and Adélies (the smaller ones) squabble in their rookeries ("Sounds of Antarctica," 2005).

Susan wants her students to organize their own questions, looking for commonalities and then forming their own investigative teams. She encourages them to use a metacognitive strategy:

Plan: What are we trying to do—what are our Questions and our Objectives? How will we approach our task? How will we organize our Time, Access to Resources, Working Together on Projects, Teachers' Presenting Content Lessons on Animal Behavior/Biology, and so forth?

Monitor: How well are we doing? Do we need to alter our goals and/or our resource plans?

Evaluate: How well did we do?

During students' investigations Susan will want to present structured lessons on a variety of subjects ranging from how to interpret animal behavior to survival skills (comparing penguins with other creatures that live in harsh environments like the sulfide chimneys on the ocean floor). She may also introduce artwork from Antarctica, perhaps showing pictures of beautiful water colors drawn by Dr. Edward A. Wilson of Scott's last expedition, found mostly in copies of Scott's books about the discovery expedition (1901–1904; *Discovery*) and his last expedition (1910–1912; *Scott's Last Expedition*).

Susan may also want to introduce the literature of south polar exploration by sharing with her students some of the most magnificent and poignant journal entries from Scott's diaries, especially those entries in 1912 of his last journey from the South Pole back to his hut at Cape Evans at McMurdo Sound. As everybody knows, he and his four companions (Wilson among them) failed to reach home base and perished out on the Ross Ice Shelf sometime in March of 1912 during raging blizzards that halted their progress. These diary entries are fascinating and may encourage a young group of budding scientists and adventurers to start their own journals.

She may also want to include lessons that help her students distinguish between fact and inference or value judgment, especially when accessing Internet sources; how to summarize and avoid plagiarism; how to draw reasonable conclusions using evidence; and how to organize and make informative presentations.

What have we Learned about penguins in Antarctica?

Here, again, Susan has a wonderful opportunity for students to share their learnings in culminating projects using a wide variety of formats and different talents and intelligences. Students can use oral reports, dramatizations, and news broadcasts from various rookeries around Ross Island, for example, Cape Crozier. They can write survival stories and include some artwork, pictures that will help students demonstrate their understandings in alternative fashions. And, of course, some of her teams will be sharing their suggested proposals to help preserve the penguins' natural habitat, which is already being affected because of the widening holes in the ozone layer over Antarctica.

Stop and Think

 How would you encourage students to culminate their investigations? What kinds of sharing of knowledge experiences would you suggest?

How will we Apply what we have learned about penguins in Antarctica?

Susan discusses with her students how what they have learned applies to the next science unit, to other subjects, and to their lives beyond school (here, students who investigated negative effects of the depletion of the ozone layer on penguins, for example, will have much to say!).

If they have read Scott's journal entries, they will connect to how such writings can be fun and helpful in their own lives.

What new Questions do we have following our inquiry?

Some students ask, "Why won't all countries reduce the use of CFCs? How will penguins survive?"

Susan's students enjoy this unit because they love animals, and penguins offer an amazing array of fascinating information, such as their capacity to hold their breath for twenty minutes while they dive to 1,400 feet for food and the fact that the larger of the species, the Emperors, lay their eggs in the dead of the Antarctic winter when it gets ragingly cold!

SHIFT IN CONTROL

This inquiry strategy is based largely on research by Dewey (1933), who said thinking begins when teachers encounter some perplexity, some doubt or difficulty; by Sigel (Sigel, Copple, & Saunders, 1984), who asserted that these doubts are the beginning of inquiry; and McCombs (1991), who strongly stated, "Students need to have choice and support for autonomy that can lead them to understand the responsibilities and benefits of their agency [control of own thinking] and the value of self-regulated learning strategies" (p. 10). When teachers allow students to take part in making decisions about what and how to study, they are helping them learn skills to identify, analyze, and solve their own problems. This paves the way for students to become more independent learners.

NOTE

1. All names of educators and students have been changed.

What's My Thinking Now

Reflection

Comments

Questions

CHAPTER 6

Student-Directed Inquiry

STUDENTS CONDUCT INDEPENDENT INQUIRIES

What does a teacher do when one or a small group of students poses a question they really want to work on? The question is not one that the whole class needs to research, yet the students have their curiosity aroused. If possible, it's important to afford these students an opportunity to find their own answers—to conduct PBL (problem-based learning) on their own.

Stop and Think

 What can you do to foster independent student inquiry, and under what conditions can you encourage such an inquiry project?

DEFINING STUDENT-DIRECTED INQUIRY

Student-directed inquiry is just what its name implies. Students work more on their own than under a teacher's guidance within an ongoing unit or as an extension thereof. Teachers might call this independent study, because students, one or more, are defining their own issues and setting their research agenda separately from the class. They are still under the teacher's supervision, of course, but the whole class might be engaged in other learning experiences. In effect, students might be considered as acting like independent entrepreneurs within a large corporation.

During such work they can build on the KWHLAQ and O-T-Q strategies (see Chapter 5) to conduct more independent research.

WHEN STUDENT-DIRECTED INQUIRY IS APPROPRIATE

Teachers know that their students are ready for independent inquiry when the group is very diverse, including some with the kinds of independent thinking and acting abilities needed to accomplish the task. These students must possess the maturity level required to work more or less on their own, to work within a structure they create (or the teacher creates with them), and to monitor their own progress with careful but not overbearing supervision from the teacher.

Another sign is when, in the course of pursuing the KWHLAQ or O-T-Q strategies (or one that is more traditional), one or more students have a real interest that can be accommodated by such a project. Independent inquiry is also helpful when one or more students might benefit from what is often called extra credit, completing an assignment over and above what is required for all other students.

Deciding when it is appropriate for students to conduct independent inquiry may not be too difficult, but teachers need a strategy to guide students through the process.

Stop and Think

 Think of a unit of study you completed with a group of students. Did any students who possessed the maturity to work independently raise any questions that they could have explored with a small group of other students?

A STRATEGY TO FOLLOW

As mentioned in Chapter 5, the overall metacognitive strategy of Planning, Monitoring, and Evaluating is an excellent approach in situations where students will be more or less on their own (see Figure 6.1). Teachers want students to be aware of their own thinking and to work to become more and more in control of their own thought and work processes. Teachers need to help students continually reflect on their own progress because they will be engaged in other learning experiences (see Figure 6.2).

Plan

To begin student-directed inquiry, students must first clearly identify questions they wish to research. The teacher needs to help students analyze a subject to find those elements that are most important and/or of greatest interest to them. This can take some time and effort on the students' part; it is an important intellectual process, one requiring good analytical skills. Students can use a concept map to web out all aspects of the question or topic they want to research, and use this overview as a picture in which they might not only see

PLAN, MONITOR, AND EVALUATE

Planning

What are our questions?

How will we organize time and access to resources to find answers?

How will we plan for sharing findings and conducting self-assessments?

What do we think we will learn?

Monitor

How well are we doing?

Are we working according to plan?

What is surprising and why?

What new questions are we asking?

Evaluate

What were the most important ideas we learned?

What did we learn about inquiry, ourselves, and others?

Where and how can we use these new ideas?

What new questions do we have?

Figure 6.1

Figure 6.2 Metacognition

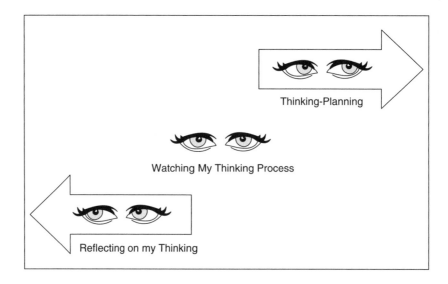

relationships but identify those elements that are most significant and fascinating.

These are some questions students can ask themselves to begin the planning process:

- What is my original question?
- Why do I think it is important?
- How can I organize my time, access to and sharing of resources, and plans to share findings?
- What do I think I will find out/learn?
- What are my hypotheses about the topic and upon what prior knowledge or assumptions am I basing them?

Notes on these concerns might provide the students with an opportunity to identify clearly what they are basing their inquiry on, those underlying domains of knowledge and assumptions under which they may be operating.

Another way students can lay out a research plan is to use the KWHLAQ strategy (see Chapter 5):

K   What do we think we **Know** about the subject?

W   What do we **Want/Need** to find out about it?

H   **How** will we go about finding out?

L   What do we expect to **Learn**? What have we **Learned**?

A   How will we **Apply** what we have learned to other subjects? to our personal lives? to our next projects?

Q   What new **Questions** do we have following our inquiry?

As with larger groups conducting an inquiry project, this strategy provides a structure for the students' inquiry. At some point investigators need to answer each of these questions during a planning (KWH), monitoring, and evaluating (LAQ) process.

Stop and Think

 Are there students in your current class who are ready for this type of independent student inquiry? How would you help them carry out this initial planning step?

Monitor

A good way to help the students self-monitor their research is to have them keep Reflective Journals and report on progress weekly. What do students put in their journals? Students need to write reflections on what they think and feel. This reflective process is called metacognition (Barell, 1995; Fogarty, 1994).

As information is gathered there are numerous opportunities for students to reflect on the meaning of data. The following are some questions students can ask themselves and answer in their Reflective Journals:

- How well am I/are we doing?
- Am I/are we working according to my/our plan?
- Does the information match my/our expectations?
- What is surprising and why?
- What is frustrating or causing me/us difficulty and why?
- Am I/are we learning things that cause me/us to rethink my/our original question? Why?
- Are there new questions I/we need to research? Are there other areas to research?
- What am I/are we learning about researching this topic? about myself/ourselves as researchers? about working collaboratively with others?

These notes begin reflection not just on the topic at hand but on the process of conducting an inquiry project (see Figure 6.3). It's important for students to begin reflecting on how they gather and interpret information, on the meanings they are creating, and on the implications thereof. Why is this important? As students march through a long, investigative process, they do so in twists and turns. Research is not a clearly linear process without potholes or storms. When students continually reflect on the decisions they have had to make along the way, they bring those decisions to conscious awareness and then, teachers hope, they can become more intelligent about their choices. Students can control their own learning (Swartz & Perkins, 1989).

Furthermore, and perhaps even more important, students need to become more aware of what McCombs (1991) refers to as "the self as agent." That is, become aware that it is I who controls what goes on in my head and that if negative thoughts enter, such as, "Oh, this is just too difficult for me," then I can say,

EXAMPLES FROM STUDENTS' REFLECTIVE JOURNALS

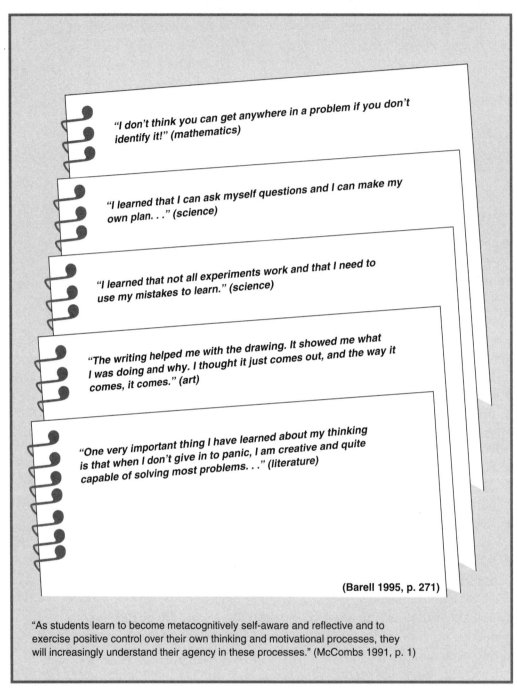

"I don't think you can get anywhere in a problem if you don't identify it!" (mathematics)

"I learned that I can ask myself questions and I can make my own plan. . ." (science)

"I learned that not all experiments work and that I need to use my mistakes to learn." (science)

"The writing helped me with the drawing. It showed me what I was doing and why. I thought it just comes out, and the way it comes, it comes." (art)

"One very important thing I have learned about my thinking is that when I don't give in to panic, I am creative and quite capable of solving most problems. . ." (literature)

(Barell 1995, p. 271)

"As students learn to become metacognitively self-aware and reflective and to exercise positive control over their own thinking and motivational processes, they will increasingly understand their agency in these processes." (McCombs 1991, p. 1)

Figure 6.3

"No, I can accomplish this task and do it well." The self as agent has the function of "overseeing, regulating, and understanding the operation of the whole self-system" (McCombs, 1991, p. 7). People create their negative thoughts (and their positive ones), and they can alter their thoughts if they choose.

Some elements in the Reflective Journal can be shared with the class or with a group of other students. One of the most exciting aspects of challenging students to engage in this more independent kind of research is that teachers get to work with them during and after the process to elicit the kinds of information suggested as appropriate for their Reflective Journals. By helping them become more reflective about their own work, teachers lead students toward greater confidence and control of their own learning processes.

Stop and Think

 How would you monitor the progress of the students you identified in the planning stage? Would you use Reflective Journals? What types of questions would you have the students answer? How often would you check the journals? What other ways would you monitor your students' progress?

Evaluate

Once a project has been completed there are many ways of challenging students to reflect on the experience. This is the "L" part of the KWHLAQ process; teachers can engage in it publicly or in journals (see Chapter 5). Journals might be more appropriate for independent researchers. Here are some writing stems that students must answer in either their presentations or in their journals:

- What were the most important ideas I learned about the topic?
- What surprised me most? Why?
- How can I relate these ideas to others within this and other units?
- What didn't I find out? Why?
- What did I learn about the process of inquiry: about posing a question and researching it? (This question can focus on difficulties, surprises, unanticipated outcomes, and such areas as time management and the process of reflection itself.)
- What might I do differently next time and why?

Part of the evaluation process includes students' being able to apply what was learned—the "A" in the KWHLAQ strategy (see Chapter 5). Application is a process that allows students to take what they think they know and transfer it to other, often novel, situations. This process can be very difficult and is often used as an assessment strategy. If students can describe how, for example, they would use the concept of checks and balances in a family situation, and their transfer fits logically and makes sense, then teachers have an idea that they understand the concept. Teachers challenge students to ask themselves these questions (Fogarty, 1989):

- How can I use what I have learned here in other areas of academic life? in my personal life?
- When might I have used such strategies/concepts/skills?

From these questions, students move to the last phase of the inquiry project, "What new questions have I found?" This last step in the KWHLAQ strategy helps students understand that inquiry is an ongoing process, continuing into other subjects and areas outside of school.

Stop and Think

How would you evaluate the students you identified in the planning and monitoring stages? Would you have them report their findings to the rest of the class? Or would you have them discuss their reflections in journals or among themselves?

SAMPLE UNITS[1]

The following sample units are divided into three sections. Once again, the teachers are composites of actual teachers who use these strategies. The first section walks through the Plan, Monitor, and Evaluate strategy that Deborah used with her elementary school class. The next two sections give several examples of how teachers at the middle and high school levels directed their students in independent research.

SAMPLE UNIT: MOUNTAIN REGIONS

Grade level: Elementary School

Model: Plan, Monitor, and Evaluate

Deborah has several students in her fifth-grade class who are interested in the unit Anne Marie conducted on mountain regions (see Chapter 4). They took an interest in the geologic formations known as plate tectonics when investigating the differences between the Appalachian and Rocky Mountains and now want to pursue more questions on that topic on their own.

They are good students, two boys and two girls, and they would like to venture off on their own to find out what they can about this phenomenon.

Deborah has no qualms about letting them work independently within an existing unit or for extra credit. She has these students follow the Plan, Monitor, and Evaluate strategy, incorporating the elements of the KWHLAQ strategy (see Chapter 5). Since the students have used the KWHLAQ strategy before, they know what the letters stand for and how to work toward resolutions.

Plan

Deborah sits down after school with her young researchers and reviews what they did in the mountain unit, assessing the depth of their understanding of essential concepts. She checks to make sure everyone understands the various steps of the KWHLAQ. She also reviews the importance of planning, monitoring, and evaluating. Once she is confident that they understand the structure and they have set a reasonable time line for their work, she asks if there are any questions. Here are some of their questions:

Students: Can we have time during school to work on this?

Deborah: Yes. [Deborah must incorporate this into her lesson in a way that will not be unfair to the other students.]

Students: Will this count on our report cards?

Deborah: Absolutely!

Students: Can we divide up the work and each report on separate things?

Deborah: How would you do it? [Deborah wants to make sure that the work is distributed evenly among the students.]

Once these kinds of issues are resolved, the students agree that they will start at home with their own concept maps reflecting what they already know about plate tectonics and what their curiosities are. Then tomorrow they can go to the library, pool their ideas, and organize themselves into an investigative team that has varied objectives and ways of getting information.

When the students are ready, Deborah looks over their completed concept maps and the questions they wish to pursue on their own. She checks their questions in a fifteen-minute discussion while some students are off at special classes and others are working on another project. Here are some of their questions:

- How do we know that plates move across our planet? What makes them move?
- What were continents like millions of years ago? What was Pangaea? Gondwanaland?
- Who were the really important scientists doing the work and how did they make these discoveries?
- How do plate tectonics affect animal life?

Deborah likes all these questions and spends some time helping them clarify and focus on an essential question or two (e.g., "How do we learn about plate tectonics and their effects upon our lives today?"). Then she suggests students work on the "H" of the KWHLAQ strategy: How will you go about finding answers? This is a major portion of their making a plan that they can then monitor and evaluate. Deborah ensures that they include personnel resources such as scientists who live in the community and/or work at the local college. She also makes certain that they can all access the wealth of resources on the Internet.

Monitor

As students set forth on their own, Deborah makes sure that they find time to meet and share their findings and that they closely monitor their progress in

Thinking Journals. Periodically, she asks to read their journals, wanting very much to provide assistance where she can. Deborah realizes these students are very capable of independence, but she wants them to know that she is interested in their work.

Evaluate

Toward the end of their research, Deborah sits down with her students and they discuss what their findings are and how they wish to share them with the rest of the class. This is an important phase of any kind of research, because Deborah, like all teachers, wants everyone to benefit from their work.

"How might you share your findings?" she asks, after they have disclosed many of their ideas and exciting research. The following are some of the students' responses:

Tommy: Well, we could draw charts that show how the plates move, all about subduction and the mid-Atlantic ridge . . . even what makes earthquakes.

Andrea: I'd like to write it all out in a story, about how the animal fossils tell us stuff about how the continents were all tied in together at Pangaea, you know?

Tiffany: We could interview the scientists, like in a TV program—like *60 Minutes* or *Dateline NBC*.

Richard: Why don't we get the class to act out the plates, you know, some be the continents and others be the Atlantic or Pacific plates?

They have lots of ideas. One thing Deborah wants to make sure of is that they summarize their findings in a more organized manner, regardless of the kinds of alternative assessments they engage in. She also wants to make sure that their sharings demonstrate their understanding of the research. Deborah does not want students to get caught up in a dramatization, for example, and lose sight of what it demonstrates. She has seen that too often.

Everyone agrees that there will be the following:

- Presentations where each researcher will engage in a demonstration of understanding and entertain questions afterward
- Opportunities for researchers to discuss what they have learned about scientific research and their own methods of inquiry; how they might apply their findings and their new questions

Following these experiences, Deborah will ask the researchers to summarize their learnings, applications, and new questions in their journals. They have done a lot of work and need not write out a lengthy paper. Informality is what they wanted from the beginning. Deborah tries to keep it fun, meaningful, and responsible!

Deborah hopes that this small task force conducting independent research will lead to enriched learning for all. One possibility is that more students will want to form investigative teams in the future. This will, of course, be possible as students mature during the year and become more responsible for their own learning. Another possibility is that this original team will generate some good and useable learning strategies for future units. They might identify important questions for all researchers to keep in mind:

- What are the important ideas/conclusions here?
- How do we know they are valid/true/reasonable?
- What evidence supports the conclusions?
- Who disagrees with these ideas or thinks about the information from a different perspective?
- Are there any biases?
- Do we need to define our terms?
- Are there other possible conclusions/interpretations?

Deborah knows that critical thinking is an important part of doing research and these kinds of questions can be very helpful no matter what topics the students are studying.

MIDDLE SCHOOL UNITS

The following are several examples of how middle school teachers incorporate student-directed inquiry into their lessons.

Jeff's seventh graders are working on the local ecology in science. He has taken them down to the local stream to observe and test the water. They have visited several recycling facilities and are reading about the causes and effects of global warming in their textbook. Several students want to investigate the depletion of the ozone layer over Antarctica. Jeff provides them with space, time, and access to resources (especially the Internet) to investigate this potentially damaging phenomenon. He uses the Plan, Monitor, and Evaluate strategy, incorporating elements of the KWHLAQ model, as Deborah did with her students.

Beth's eighth graders have spent the seventh grade working together on a long-range interdisciplinary project called Adopt a Town (Barell, 1995). As a result they are good researchers and can work well on their own. Some of their topics include:

- Fitness for the elderly
- Cosmetic testing on animals
- What are the limits of community development?

Ellen's students are reading *Hatchet,* by Gary Paulsen. This is a captivating story of a young boy's struggle for survival in the wilderness of Canada. Several students want to do independent projects on survival skills and how they can be used in various environments: in arctic regions, at sea, and in the desert.

Chuck's social studies students are studying early hominids, and some students would like to dig more deeply into the field of paleoanthropology. They

especially want to search Internet sources for what they want to know, because they live far away from the major metropolitan museums. They are intrigued by fossils such as Lucy and want to know more about the differences between *Homo sapiens* and Neanderthals.

HIGH SCHOOL UNITS

The following are several examples of how high school teachers incorporate student-directed inquiry into their lessons.

April's students in world history and cultures are investigating the cultures of Africa. She designs her unit so students can select any number of independent research projects, focused on a specific country, era, or style of art.

Bill's literature students are reading Shakespearean comedies and tragedies. He wants them to engage in independent research after having read at least one play. They have the whole Elizabethan era as their focus.

Michael's students are studying genetics. There are numerous issues of a bioethical nature that can be investigated, from cloning to fetal manipulation and genetic screening.

Barbara's students in upper-level mathematics courses are afforded time to research such topics as the lives of early mathematicians, current applications of calculus and trigonometry in everyday life, and the philosophy of mathematics from Plato to Newton to Einstein.

In Phyllis's Italian III and IV classes, students love to read fables. Her goal for them is to create their own story and transform it into a fable in Italian, one that can be shared with others. Students are given the option to work individually, in pairs, or in groups. After reading the fable, students can analyze the characters, reflect on the language, share a personal story that relates to the fable, change the dialogue to a narrative format, role play, create a report to present to the rest of the class, or reflect on learning by completing concept maps, Venn diagrams, or writing in journals (Pizzolato, 1996). Finally, students can create their own fables.

OPPORTUNITIES FOR INDEPENDENT RESEARCH

These are just a few units that can provide students with wonderful opportunities for independent research, reporting, and reflection. There are so many rich possibilities in all courses for independent PBL that teachers are limited only by their imaginations and their openness to alternative course requirements, structures, and uses of time.

NOTE

1. All names of educators and students have been changed.

What's My Thinking Now

Reflection

Comments

Questions

CHAPTER 7

Multidisciplinary Approaches

WHY THEY ARE IMPORTANT FOR PBL

Teachers working alone in their own classrooms are sometimes fascinated and amazed when they find out what their colleagues are doing. "I never knew you were teaching those kinds of topics," said one language arts teacher to her colleagues in science and mathematics after spending some quality professional development time with members of her interdisciplinary team. This may sound surprising for teachers who are supposed to be working together, collaborating on common topics. But the reality is that even if teachers teach in a school originally designed for interdisciplinary work in teams that have common planning times, there is no assurance that such teamwork will take place. Even with quality time to plan, this kind of interdisciplinary planning is challenging. One teacher noted, "This is the most difficult work I've had to do!"

So why even think about collaborating on units of instruction? Learning in schools tends to be rather fragmented, with students learning information in nearly watertight compartments that have little connectedness across them. Meaningful learning results from the connections and relationships discovered and created among the myriad pieces of information one receives. In other words, learning can become more meaningful and, thereby, long-lasting if students are successful in relating and making connections to knowledge, skills, and attitudes among their different subjects.

Jacob Bronowski (1965), noted scientist and interpreter of literature, wrote, "All science is the search for unity in hidden likenesses" (p. 13). Newton saw gravity as the connecting and unifying concept between the moon and the falling apple. Bronowski also spoke of imagination as an "opening of the system so that it shows new connections" (Bronowski, 1978, p. 109). This means that insight and perhaps knowledge can result from making connections among things that seem very different, and this is where multidisciplinary studies come in.

Giving students the opportunity to seek and find relationships among different subjects helps students make their learnings more meaningful and significant. It is the connections that students make, not those imposed by the teacher, that are the most important and the ones most remembered. The connections students make are the ones likely to be stored in long-term memory, ready to use when needed in future problem-solving situations.

Divergent events (complex, robust phenomena) are by nature open to multiple points of view (hence, the term "boundaryless"). Any questions about the federal judiciary or Congress involve not only history but also economics, philosophy, literature, and perhaps mathematics and science as well. Questions about ecology involve not only science but also history, the social sciences, art, and literature. The more students are engaged in thinking deeply about important problematic situations, the more they need help to analyze these problems from a variety of different points of view and to draw reasoned conclusions.

There are several different ways to encourage problem-based learning (PBL) with interdisciplinary thinking, some that involve one teacher alone in the classroom and others that involve teachers planning cooperatively together.

Stop and Think

 Why do you think it's important for students to make connections among all subjects? What are you currently doing in your classroom to foster students' creating their own interdisciplinary relationships?

ONE TEACHER IN THE CLASSROOM

Even without the luxury of working with a team of teachers that meets regularly to map out interdisciplinary units, there is a lot that teachers can do in their own classrooms. Through a variety of strategies, teachers can challenge students to make connections and to seek the kinds of relationships that Bronowski (1965) spoke of. Teachers can challenge students to reach beyond the restrictions of the classroom walls to make connections among the subjects they are learning.

Strategies for the Teacher Working Alone

The following are some of the strategies used in Chapters 4 through 6. Now teachers need to look at them for their interdisciplinary value from the viewpoint of one teacher working alone in his or her classroom, where collaboration with other faculty is not the norm.

KWHLAQ

When students create a concept map during the "What do we think we Know?" phase of KWHLAQ (see Chapter 5), teachers can stress students' relating one subject to another. This is an attempt to break down the classroom walls that artificially separate the subjects students are learning.

The key idea here, of course, is found in the word *relate.* When students relate one thing to another, or make connections, they are seeking and finding similarities; they are identifying essential characteristics that things or phenomena have in common. The act of making connections or relating is what makes something meaningful; therefore, making meanings is a process of seeking many different kinds of connections. When teachers help make these connections at the beginning of a unit, they are transferring information to the new unit. This process will become more meaningful for students when they place an idea within an already familiar context. This is what learning is—relating the new to the known.

For example, there are many different connections students can make with the word *cell:* cells in human bodies, jail cells, cells where monks live, cells in spreadsheet technology, beehive cells, a communist party cell, cellular phones, and probably many more. The more connections students can make for the word cell, the more meaning the word may have for them. The more extensive the set of references to a word is, the more meaningful it is (Johnson, 1975).

Take another example: If a teacher is investigating the topic of pioneer women, how many different subject areas can he or she identify that relate to the topic? The teacher may have ideas in these areas: history, literature (e.g., Willa Cather, diaries of women adventurers), environmental studies (e.g., uses of land, conservation), science (e.g., diet, nutrition, farming, disease prevention), philosophy/religion (e.g., outlook on life, self-determination), law/legal issues (e.g., property ownership, male domination, inheritance laws), and so forth (see Figure 7.1).

Figure 7.1   Pioneer Women Concept Map

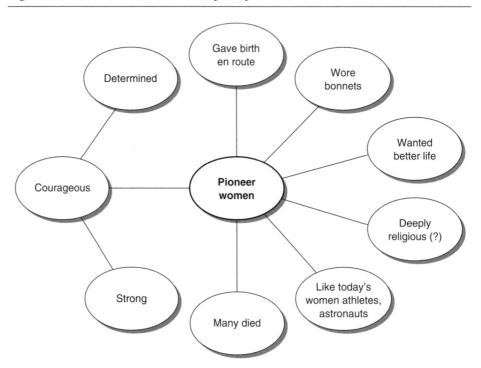

When students engage in the "K" of the KWHLAQ, they transfer in their preexistent knowledge, and this, of course, comes from a wide variety of sources, not just school. In the early stages of inquiry, students begin to relate what they think they already know. Then in searching for relationships and patterns, they make the information of their initial concept maps more meaningful, and teachers must make this an explicit element in their teaching, by saying, for example, "Searching for connections is one way of making ideas more meaningful." Thus, preserving students' original and subsequent concept maps helps us all see how they have developed the meaningfulness of significant concepts.

Research Problems

Teachers can conduct research into problematic areas that involve more than one area of study. If the teacher's central question is, "How did the pioneers survive?" the areas of history, science, philosophy/religion, and perhaps law can be investigated. In other words, teachers frame their central or essential question so that it crosses subject-matter lines, making it more complex, robust, and fascinating.

Thinking/Inquiry Journals

Teachers can use Thinking/Inquiry Journals to encourage students to make connections among different subjects—to search for relationships. Students can use Thinking/Inquiry Journals in their investigations to make notes of the different areas they are learning about. For example, students can continually relate what they are finding out about explorers to what they already know in different subject areas. The following sentence stems can assist students in this type of thinking:

- This reminds me of. . . . (how explorers like Lewis and Clark survived on their Northwest expedition)
- I can relate/connect this information to. . . . (the idea of preserving resources to my use of breathing during cross-country racing)
- I wonder how this relates to. . . . (their lack of preparation for diseases relates to our present-day safeguards)
- This makes me think of. . . . (their struggles make me think of the astronauts and the space program)

Students' Current Understandings

When students report on what they know, they will not say, "Here's something from history or science," and so forth. What teachers can do is write their ideas on the board and help students identify the subjects they have transferred information from for this new study. In the pioneer women unit, teachers might ask students to identify information they know from history, science, literature, and so on:

- They left from the eastern part of the United States in search of better farmland (history)

- They encountered many diseases and some died (history/science)
- They wrote diaries describing their adventures (language arts)
- If they were to survive, they had to find food in lots of different places and learn to prepare very different kinds of meals (science)

Teacher Questions and Responses

Teacher questions and responses challenge students to search for connections to prior knowledge from other subjects. For example, when discussing a major idea, teachers can ask some of the following questions:

- What can you relate this to?
- What does this make you think of?
- How do these facts connect or relate to other areas you are studying?

The new questions can then follow multidisciplinary lines, and teachers and students commence the cycle over again. Some questions for the pioneer women unit might be the following:

- What kinds of diseases did they suffer from and how could their illnesses have been prevented? (science)
- What do their diaries tell us about why they left good homes in the East? (language arts)

These questions can lead to wonderful opportunities for students to connect current topics of discussion to their prior knowledge. Some of these will be very concrete and literal, such as relating force in physics to use of force in history; others will be far more subtle, creative, and different from anything the teacher could have predicted.

Now, what do teachers do when students make connections that seem strange, incomprehensible, and totally original? How do they respond? Here is another opportunity to probe students' thinking with questions:

- How did you make that connection?
- What similarities do you see between these two experiences, subjects, or topics?
- Can you help us understand how you figured out that relationship?

Questions such as these honor students' contributions and communicate teachers' desire to understand the complexities of students' thinking. Is there anything teachers can do with the responses besides listen to them? One thing teachers might be able to do is isolate any strategies students are using, such as visualizing, classifying by significant elements (some of which are not immediately evident), making inferences based on hidden likenesses, challenging assumptions, and using feelings to make connections. Teachers can display these strategies around the room for use by other students after they have analyzed them so everyone understands how they are used.

Reconceptualizing the Individual Role

This approach of one teacher working alone provides teachers with opportunities they can use whether or not they are a member of a designated interdisciplinary team. Teachers need to reconceptualize their roles from that of a single teacher working alone to that of a much larger team of teachers working to help students make their learnings more meaningful. All teachers can work toward this objective by using some of the strategies mentioned above. If teachers are fortunate enough to work with one or more other teachers, they can make more elaborate plans to help students integrate their understandings.

Stop and Think

 Now that you have read through all the strategies for one teacher working alone, which strategies have you used in your classroom? Which strategies do you think you can implement at the beginning of your next unit of study?

TEACHER COLLABORATION

There are probably many ways for students to make connections among all of their learnings. Two ways in particular require that at least two teachers work together. Very often this occurs in middle schools where teams of teachers from the major subject areas design and implement interdisciplinary units. Teachers at elementary and high school levels also engage in challenging students to investigate a subject from a variety of points of view. This is the definition of "interdisciplinary" used here.

Strategies for Teacher Collaboration

The first strategy, focusing on integrating thinking, helps students make connections conceptually and on providing them with what Tyler (1949) calls an integrative thread. Such a thread can be woven through the curriculum, especially from early to later grades, in the form of intellectual skills such as problem solving. The second strategy, integrating concepts, focuses on approaching robust, complex human dilemmas from many different points of view.

Focus on Integrating Thinking

One of the easiest ways for teachers to collaborate and integrate their subjects is to use the threaded model. The threaded model shows how specific thought processes, such as inquiry, problem solving, and critical thinking, can become the integrative threads woven throughout several subjects.

For example, during recent collaborations with middle school teachers on interdisciplinary teams, it became very evident that each teacher was challenging students to think along similar lines in a unit on early hominids:

Science Teacher:	We always start with the scientific method: identifying a problem, gathering data, stating a hypothesis, conducting an experiment, reviewing data, and drawing conclusions.
Language Arts Teacher:	Well, we can use a variation of that in literature. After students read Jack London's "To Build a Fire," we can work on their conclusions about the protagonist's character.
Social Studies Teacher:	Same in my subject. Students have to be able to draw inferences from, say, the archeological data about early humans. They will scientifically examine a number of artifacts, not jump to conclusions, and stick to direct observations first and then draw inferences and conclusions.
Math Teacher:	Well, that's like problem solving, trying to figure out how to solve something. We need to gather data and then analyze it before we use a formula.

See Figures 7.2 and 7.3 for ways to graphically illustrate threading the curricula.

Stop and Think

 Take a moment to identify the crucial thinking processes you want your students to engage in while they are learning a particular subject. Check off one or more from the list below:

- Identify problems
- Ask good questions
- Generate alternative solutions
- Select good solutions
- Implement and reflect
- Critical listening/viewing
- Make good decisions
- Think critically:
  - o Identify important information
  - o Seek relationships
  - o Challenge assumptions
  - o Create analogies, models

- o Differentiate fact and inferences
- o Take the opposite point of view
- o Draw conclusions or inferences
- Think creatively:
  - o Find new problems
  - o Create novel solutions
  - o Create metaphors, analogies
- Reflect metacognitively:
  - o Plan, Monitor, and Evaluate

Which of these processes do you think you and your colleagues can agree on as threads woven through your entire school year's curriculum? Which can you teach directly? Which can you assess at the beginning, middle, and end of the school year?

Figure 7.2   Integrating Critical Thinking and Problem Solving

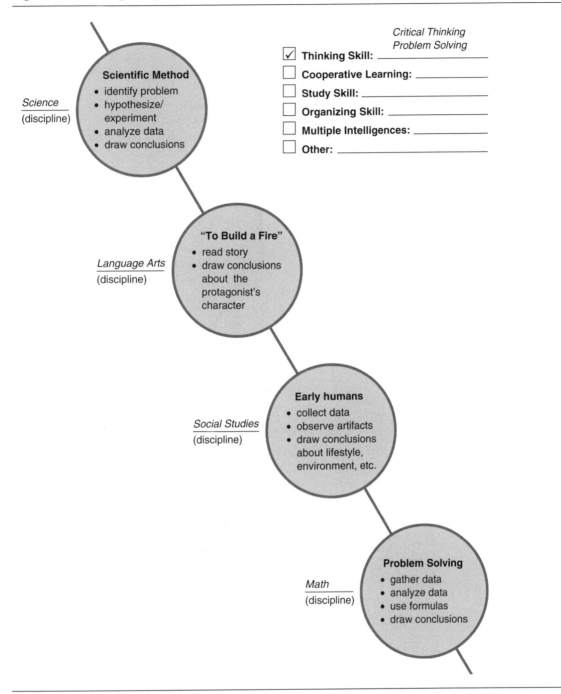

SOURCE: Adapted from *The Mindful School: How to Integrate the Curricula,* by Robin Fogarty, 1991, p. 71.

By focusing on one or two essential thought processes, teachers build a solid foundation for students' learning based on the principles of integration.

Teachers can also focus on certain dispositions, such as persistence, confidence, respect for and openness to each other's ideas, taking risks, responsibility for one's own actions, and cooperating with others. Such concern for interpersonal relations is another foundational element in developing good instruction as well as interdisciplinary units.

Figure 7.3   Integrative Threads

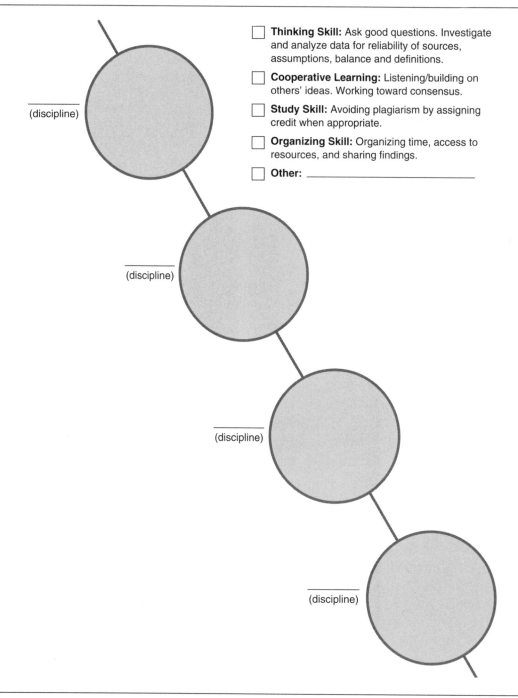

(discipline)

☐ **Thinking Skill:** Ask good questions. Investigate and analyze data for reliability of sources, assumptions, balance and definitions.

☐ **Cooperative Learning:** Listening/building on others' ideas. Working toward consensus.

☐ **Study Skill:** Avoiding plagiarism by assigning credit when appropriate.

☐ **Organizing Skill:** Organizing time, access to resources, and sharing findings.

☐ **Other:** _____

(discipline)

(discipline)

(discipline)

SOURCE: Adapted from *The Mindful School: How to Integrate the Curricula,* by Robin Fogarty, 1991, p. 71.

Stop and Think

List some dispositions you would like to focus on. How would you emphasize any one of them (or other dispositions, such as curiosity, fairness, deliberateness, passion for objectivity, truth, etc.) during the first couple of days of school? What can you do to model good dispositions and behaviors, set up controlled experiences that focus on them, or use others' experiences for these purposes?

Integration by intellectual, social, and physical skills can be a very practical way to establish a firm foundation for a meaningful education.

Focus on Integrating Concepts

Focusing on integrating concepts is more complex. The objective is to engage students in a multidisciplinary problematic situation and to have them work comfortably within the complex situation. For example, if an interdisciplinary team decides to research the concept of early human beings, the team needs to find a central question or problematic situation, a robust, discrepant event or experience that will stimulate students' inquiry.

In one middle school, the science, language arts, and history teachers found ways to integrate their subjects around concepts such as survival skills, survival tools that were built from stone and bone, and the discovery and uses of fire. Jack London's classic tale, "To Build a Fire," provided a keen example of the perils people still encounter today. These perils are similar to those depicted in programs about early hominids on PBS's *Nova* (e.g., "In Search of Human Origins," 1997). The central problem or question was not too difficult to arrive at: How did early humans survive and what can we learn from them to help us survive today? (see Figures 7.4 and 7.5).

It may take some teams a little longer to find that problem or question around which to focus the unit. One middle school team wanted to deal with students' poor interpersonal relationships, because they noticed their seventh graders engaging in a lot of verbal and physical disputes. The science, math, language arts, and geography teachers figured out how they could each deal with relationships among numbers and variables, persons, and persons in relationship to their environment. But nothing really came together, until they had their essential question or problem, and that question turned out to be, "How can we foster positive relationships among our students?" Interestingly, the math teacher, who had the most difficult time figuring out how her subject related to this topic, ended up by saying, "And my role is to teach students how to analyze a problem in relationships and then start the problem-solving process" (see Figure 7.6).

In each team's case, the essential question or focusing dilemma helped members design the learning experiences in each subject and those experiences common between subjects.

The Missing "Grout"

Research suggests that when it comes to teaming there is a tendency for each teacher to work within his or her own self-constructed teaching style and intellectual framework (Elmore, Peterson, & McCarthey, 1996). Teachers hold onto what they know and how they teach without too much sharing of these

INTEGRATING CONCEPTS FOR HOMINIDS

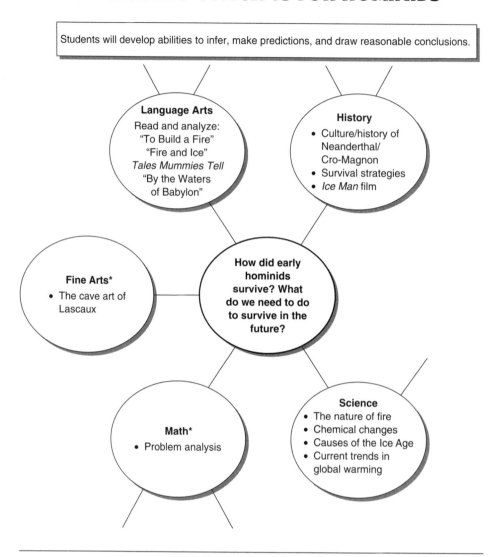

Students will develop abilities to infer, make predictions, and draw reasonable conclusions.

Language Arts
Read and analyze:
"To Build a Fire"
"Fire and Ice"
Tales Mummies Tell
"By the Waters
of Babylon"

History
• Culture/history of
Neanderthal/
Cro-Magnon
• Survival strategies
• *Ice Man* film

Fine Arts*
• The cave art of
Lascaux

**How did early
hominids
survive? What
do we need to do
to survive in the
future?**

Math*
• Problem analysis

Science
• The nature of fire
• Chemical changes
• Causes of the Ice Age
• Current trends in
global warming

Figure 7.4

SOURCE: Adapted from *The Mindful School: How to Integrate the Curricula*, Robin Fogarty, 1991, p. 59.

* Possible additions to this unit as designed by Mary Wallace, Charles Dolan, and Andrew Temme of Thomas Jefferson Middle School, Fairlawn, NJ, 1997.

domains with their colleagues. The result is that students are exposed to one teacher who uses a discovery method and another who teaches more directly. There is no guarantee that collaboration will result in teachers' using a unified teaching style in a given unit.

Another observation researchers have made is that under these conditions, when students work in teams, "knowledge [is] compartmentalized within each individual team member, rather than constructed collaboratively among [them]" (Elmore et al., 1996, p. 48). In other words, teachers are not doing what students find difficult to do—integrate several disciplines of knowledge.

Consequently, at the end of a well-thought-out unit plan involving several disciplines, teachers have observed that students did not perceive the

INTEGRATING CONCEPTS

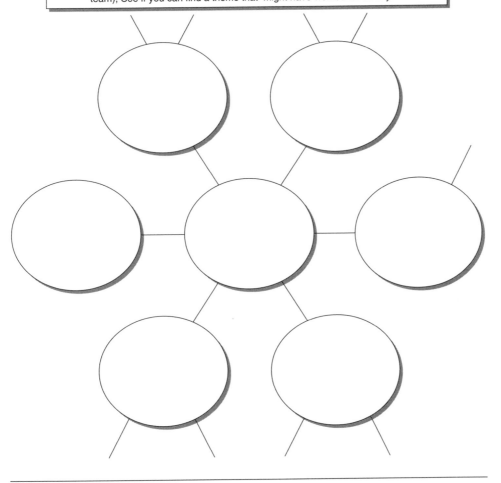

Think back to units you've Just done and, as an interdisciplinary team (or a grade-level team), See if you can find a theme that might have worked for all of you.

Figure 7.5

SOURCE: Adapted from *The Mindful School: How to Integrate the Curricula*, Robin Fogarty, 1991, p. 59.

"grout" that held it all together. Teachers had worked hard and planned good culminating experiences that involved lots of intellectual activity, but in the end they were not sure that students had made the hoped-for connections among the disciplines. For example, in units focused on conservation, each teacher had taught more or less separately (without much common planning time), with the end result that students did not have an opportunity to relate one subject to another. They did not see how the literature related to the science or to the math. Conservation was a central focus, but there was no "grout" of perceived relationships that tied all the subjects together.

Evidently, it is a new challenge for a lot of teachers to share knowledge of relationships and learn from each other. Consider a recent conclusion by one of the most astute students of school change, Michael Fullan (2001):

INTEGRATING CONCEPTS FOR RELATIONSHIPS

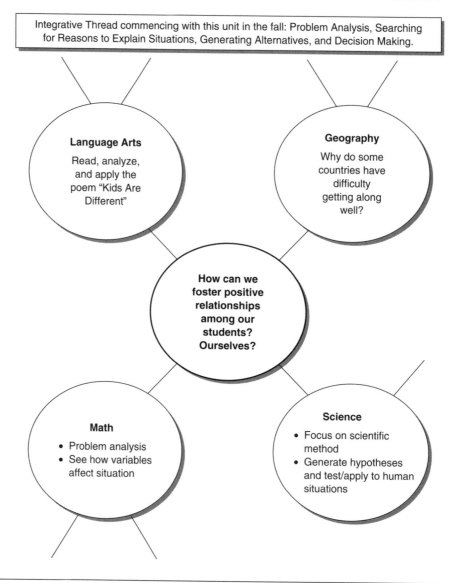

Integrative Thread commencing with this unit in the fall: Problem Analysis, Searching for Reasons to Explain Situations, Generating Alternatives, and Decision Making.

Language Arts
Read, analyze, and apply the poem "Kids Are Different"

Geography
Why do some countries have difficulty getting along well?

How can we foster positive relationships among our students? Ourselves?

Math
• Problem analysis
• See how variables affect situation

Science
• Focus on scientific method
• Generate hypotheses and test/apply to human situations

Figure 7.6

SOURCE: Adapted from *The Mindful School: How to Integrate Curricula*, Robin Fogarty, 1991, p. 29.

NOTE: This unit was designed by Diane Carrano, Paul MacDonald, Heidi Wolk, and Racquel Thompson of Thomas Jefferson Middle School, Fairlawn, NJ, 1997.

> It is one of life's great ironies: schools are in the business of teaching and learning, yet they are terrible at learning from each other. If they ever discover how to do this, their future is assured. (p. 92)

Thus, we need to think ourselves out of the narrower confines of language arts, history, math, or science. One sure way to do this is for teachers to spend focused time together. This sounds easy, but everybody knows it takes planning and time. Teachers working collaboratively can use some of the same techniques teachers working alone use:

- Use Inquiry Journals
- Foster class discussions that challenge students to integrate concepts, ideas, principles, and facts
- Use graphic organizers to help the integration process (e.g., use concept maps as homework and keep them as a permanent record of students' developing understandings)
- Give students "Integrating Time," opportunities during which they reflect on what they're learning, to seek and create connections with what they think they know in other subjects and in their personal lives (recall the Inquiry Journal stems devoted to helping students create connections, seek relationships, etc.; see Figure 2.4)
- Design culminating activities that integrate different subjects
- Ask students to integrate all subjects in their reflective summaries

Stop and Think

 List some of the ways you and your colleagues can ensure that students begin to make connections (to find and use the "grout" productively) among the different subjects you are teaching?

Assessment of the Team

If teachers and students want to gain maximum benefit from these integrative experiences, both must carry through with self-assessment. This evaluation is part of the metacognitive Plan, Monitor, and Evaluate process (see Chapter 6).

Student Assessment

During the debriefing phase, teachers need to help students reflect on their learnings to analyze what they learned:

- About relationships among subject areas (e.g., How did knowing the science of fire help them understand the culture of early human beings' survival?)
- About themselves (e.g., What new survival skills have they learned and how can they be used in their own lives?)
- About inquiry (e.g., Can they now ask better questions in a variety of situations?)

Teacher Assessment

Working collaboratively with other faculty can be the most rewarding, challenging, and difficult aspect of teaching. There is no doubt that some teams work rather smoothly and others will have their personality differences. When working with teams of teachers, it is always important to engage in reflection

after doing most of the work. Reflection should include questions such as the following:

- What did we observe about our own collaboration?
- What are we learning about our own problem solving?
- What feelings are we experiencing?
- What do we want to do differently next time and how will we go about it?

These kinds of reflections can work very well if teachers are willing to confront themselves. If they are not, it might take a while to become honest about what is transpiring. This is the same kind of self-reflection teachers ask of their students when the students engage in small group work. When a teacher asks his or her recorders to reflect on how well they worked, this is exactly what is being asked. This kind of reflection requires honesty, fortitude, and a good deal of practice. If third graders can do it, so can teachers.

If teachers really want collaboration to work, they must use their own teacher deliberations to serve as learning laboratories and to use these experiences as models for students. Teachers shouldn't expect to be perfect, only to try to identify what they do well, what they might improve on, and how they will do that. It's not easy, not for third or tenth graders or for teachers, but it is most rewarding.

CONNECT LEARNING

Whether working alone or collaboratively, it's important for teachers to help students connect what they are learning to other subjects and to areas outside of the classroom. If teachers want what their students learn to be truly meaningful, they must implement "Integrating/Connecting Time" within their PBL lessons to help students make the connections and see the relationships.

What's My Thinking Now

Reflection

Comments

Questions

CHAPTER 8

Assessment, Application, and Reflection

TESTING, SCANTRONS, AND UNDERSTANDINGS

For too long, assessment has been associated with paper-and-pencil tests that demand convergent kinds of answers. Now, with the advent of No Child Left Behind and the increasing emphasis on "high-stakes testing," assessment has in too many instances continued to be a matter of preparing for tests where students use a No. 2 pencil on a mark sense card that is read by a Scantron machine.

This is quick, efficient, and revealing of strengths and weaknesses in student achievement, but hardly representative of what students are learning: what they understand and can apply to a wide variety of in- and out-of-school situations.

Wiggins (1993) differentiates between *tests* and *assessments*. The former is a measuring device used to record information at one sitting in the form of a score. Most tests take "complex performances and divid[e] them into discrete, independent tasks that minimize the ambiguity of the result" (p. 15). As a result, asserts Wiggins, most tests tend to be indirect measures of learning and therefore inauthentic ways of evaluating performance.

An assessment, on the other hand, is designed to help both teachers and students come to agreement about what students understand, both currently and over a period of time. An assessment helps teachers examine one of the major goals of education: achieving "understanding and the habits of mind that a student becomes disposed to use" (Wiggins, 1993, p. 9). An "assessment is a comprehensive, multifaceted analysis of performance; it must be judgment-based and personal" (p. 13).

Testing is a short-term means of gathering discrete information that has limited validity in terms of helping teachers form judgments about the depth and quality of students' understanding of the complex issues, ideas, concepts, skills, and dispositions that are the core of PBL (problem-based learning).

Thus, at the culmination of individual or multidisciplinary PBL units, teachers need assessments that help them meet the demands of understanding, not merely of acquisition, storage, and retrieval of discrete pieces of information.

OBJECTIVES AND ASSESSMENTS

I vividly recall teaching *Macbeth* in high school in New York City. The class was often comprised of dramatizations, lessons on metaphors ("Life's but a walking shadow, a poor player . . ."); writing experiences ("If you were Macbeth in this situation, what would you do?"), and other assorted learning experiences.

When it came time to assess, to determine a grade for the unit, I said to myself, "What can I test these kids on? Some were here for all sessions, others were absent, and there were various interruptions."

You can immediately see what's wrong with this scenario—deciding after instruction how and what to assess of students' learning. It sounds as if I hadn't written out any objectives for this unit.

My point here is that we need to ensure that there is a close relationship between our objectives and our assessments. Assessments are designed to see what learnings have occurred and to what extent students have understood the major concepts we have derived from the curriculum and from state curriculum content standards.

Here's another scenario: You set the objective that students understand the nature of the forces impelling westward expansion of the United States in the nineteenth century. Your assessment calls for students to take a short-answer test and to create a mural of any aspect of the expansion. What difficulties do you have with this approach? (I am indebted to Grant Wiggins for suggesting this kind of scenario.)

It may be that students are excellent at rendering figures within a physical setting using paint. But does this necessarily mean they understand the economic, social, political, and religious reasons for leaving Massachusetts and setting out over the prairie and the Rocky Mountains for Oregon? What would be a better assessment of students' understandings?

WHAT ARE ALTERNATIVE, AUTHENTIC, AND PERFORMANCE ASSESSMENTS?

Students should begin to think of the culminating experience of a unit of study as more than simply a test of their knowledge in the traditional format. To do this, teachers need to engage students in thinking about the process of assessment long before the unit's conclusion. Students must become part of the planning process and, as shown below, this means becoming involved in establishing reasonable criteria with which to self-assess.

The final presentations and assessments will be the following:

Alternative: experiences that tap into students' varying ways of making content meaningful. This can, obviously, involve concepts known as

"multiple intelligences" as well as various learning and thinking styles (see Gregory & Chapman, 2002, pp. 20–26)

Authentic: related to the kinds of challenging (Levels II and III) intellectual experiences adults and students have in life beyond the classroom

Performance: demonstrating the depth and quality of understanding of central concepts

Alternative

When I taught *Othello* at Montclair State University, I wanted to give all students opportunities to share their understandings of the play in whatever ways and forms they found meaningful. I therefore said, "You may use any art form to express what you understand about the complex characters, themes, and issues in the play." There was consternation for a while, until the artist in everybody came to the fore and this is what I received:

- An original piece of music composed for viola by a member of the university orchestra
- A cartoon of Iago, full of a variety of symbols representing, among other elements of his character, the very famous speech to Othello, "Beware the green eyed monster; it doth mock the meat it feeds on."
- A lengthy poem written in free verse about Desdemona
- A few original oil paintings
- Several collages of varying complexity and aesthetic quality

There were no dance routines, no short stories, no videotapes, no panel discussions, and no models of the Globe Theater, all of which would have been excellent alternative assessments.

Alternatives are just that—alternatives to the traditional paper-and-pencil, memorize-the-material kinds of tests. They might include, if we're hooked on multiple intelligences:

- Write a play—Verbal Linguistic
- Develop a mimetic experience, or a role play—Bodily/Kinesthetic
- Compose music—Musical
- Connect ideas to nature—Naturalist
- Paint or draw a picture—Visual
- Interview others—Interpersonal
- Create a pattern—Logical
- Write in a journal—Intrapersonal (Gregory & Chapman, 2002, p. 119)

We can engage in a wide variety of such experiences, but I'm not really sure we foster any one of these "intelligences" merely by painting a picture or writing in a journal. We need more concerted efforts and reflection on the process in order to foster development.

A good example comes from Judy Frohman, second-grade teacher in Livingston, New Jersey, who assessed her students' understanding of how water, air, and solar energy can be used as forces:

Choose either air, water, or solar forces and write a paragraph describing what you have learned about that force. Include experiments we have done and remember to explain how and why the experiment worked. The more details you include the better.

She also asked students to draw a picture of a system they created. One student wrote about airplanes:

We had an airplane contest. Our airplanes flew because the air under our airplanes had a higher presher because it was skuooshed under the wing of our airplanes. The air under our airplane wanted to go to the low presher wich is the upper side of the airplane wich is above the wing.

I must admit to being quite amazed that second graders could understand the basics of Bernoulli's principle. Judy's use of experiments, contests, building of model airplanes, and then writing and drawing pictures helped her students understand the principles of flight.

In my own accessing of students' aesthetic abilities, I insisted that every artistic creation be accompanied by a detailed and reflective analysis of how the work came about. So, in the case of Craig's Iago cartoon, I learned what represented the "green-eyed monster" (Iago's eyes) and what the flower with one black petal represented as well as the one hand hidden behind his back ("I am not what I seem").

In other words, alternatives are wonderful means of tapping into the many and varied ways students can make content meaningful, but, in addition, I want a description of what it all means. Without Todd's written explanation I would not have understood his musical analogy for the entire play (see Barell, 1995, for these alternative assessments).

Authentic

Recall our previous mention of Newmann's (1996) concept of "authentic achievement" as that involving "cognitive work found in the adult world" (p. 24). This refers to those intellectual challenges found at Levels II and III of the Three-Story Intellect. For example, students would be asked to "organize, synthesize, interpret, explain or evaluate complex information in addressing a concept, problem or issue" (p. 29).

"Authentic assessment" also refers to a set of criteria developed by Grant Wiggins (1998) for assessments:

1. Students make judgments involving critical thinking and problem solving.

2. They are "realistic" in that they "replicate contexts in which a person's knowledge and abilities are 'tested' in real-world situations."

3. They "do" the subject as historians or scientists would.

4. They present their findings in such settings where they can rehearse and receive immediate, direct feedback, thereby being able to modify their conclusions (see Wiggins, 1998, p. 22).

Thus, for both Newmann and Wiggins, assessment must involve challenging students to engage in complex intellectual work, the kind found in the world beyond learning stuff from a textbook. This involves the complex task of applying concepts, ideas, principles, and skills to complex, problematic situations. For example, "How would we analyze (compare/contrast) the checks and balances within the French or British parliamentary system? What conclusions could we draw following such an analysis?"

These kinds of challenges are the real test of the depth and quality of students' understandings. This is one of the major goals of education: application of knowledge and skills to life situations. Education is for life now (as Dewey noted), not at some distant point in the future. Delaying application is one reason why so many students are so bored in class and teachers often hear, "When am I ever going to use this?"

Performing Understandings

How can students demonstrate that they understand a concept, idea, principle, skill, or disposition? If a teacher considers the concept of balance of powers, students can demonstrate their understanding with the following performance experiences:

Experiments	Poetry or Stories
Solved Problems	Interviews
Supported Decisions	News Programs
Written Reports	Dance
Dramatic Presentations	Models
Films	Metaphors
Journals/Diaries	Analogies
Collages	

All of these experiences can and should be accompanied by some form of written or spoken explanation wherein students relate to an audience the depth of their understanding of central questions and concepts (Wiggins, 1993).

These examples, however, do not go far enough. They are the structures within which students demonstrate their understanding. For example, if teachers want students to demonstrate their understanding of democracy, they can ask students to engage in a number of different and challenging intellectual tasks:

- Define (e.g., democracy is a form of government)
- Explain (e.g., give examples of how democratic governments function)
- Exemplify (e.g., present examples of one or more democracies)
- Compare and contrast (e.g., compare and contrast democratic governments with each other and with communist and fascist regimes)
- Draw conclusions (e.g., draw conclusions about comparisons and differences between democratic governments and communist and fascist regimes)
- Identify and analyze problematic situations (e.g., the conflict between rights of the individual and society at large)
- Apply (e.g., apply the concept of democracy to any emerging government in another area, such as Latin America, Africa, or Asia; analyze the strengths of these emerging governments in accordance with the characteristics of a democracy and draw your own conclusions)
- Create models, metaphors, and analogies (e.g., create a model government in a new country, a model of photosynthesis, an analogy of plate tectonics)
- Hypothesize (e.g., What would happen if certain conditions were to prevail within our own [or others'] democracies; for example, censorship of the press, curtailment of the right to freedom of assembly, growing intolerance for those who are different, etc.?)
- Generate or respond to questions (e.g., What if generals of the army made foreign policy?)
- Teach the concept (e.g., teach the concept of democracy to children in elementary school, using examples from their own lives)

LETTERS HOME AND ANALOGIES

During a professional development needs assessment meeting at her school, Barbara M'Gonigle (Dumont High School, Dumont, NJ) said, "My students can get the right answers, but they do not understand the basic concepts." They were memorizing what she and the textbook said about various mathematical concepts.

So Barbara devised a number of alternative ways to assess students' understanding of concepts, including the following:

1. Write a letter to Mom and Dad explaining in terms they can understand what we are learning. You cannot assume significant prior knowledge.

2. Create an analogy about a major concept. For example, "The Limit" in math was described as similar to a credit card maximum and a speed limit. (Barell, 1995)

Creating models, metaphors, and analogies involves comparing and contrasting, an intellectual skill we know contributes to positive achievement. It is one of the means of determining the depth and quality of students' understanding of content concepts and ideas.

These and other mental processes can and should be part of performance assessments.

Stop and Think

 Using the suggested formats for performance assessments, and one or more intellectual processes, design two different assessments for a unit you are currently working on.

How does either one of your assessments demonstrate that students do indeed understand the content of the unit (the major concepts, ideas, principles, and skills)?

Let's review how some of the units in earlier chapters might have been assessed.

Anne Marie's unit on Appalachia (Chapter 4)

Objective A: Students will determine how mountains form.

Possible Assessments: Create a project explaining mountain formation; prepare video using clips from the Internet on mountain building processes (e.g., plate subduction); write a formal paper; teach concept to younger students.

Objective B: Compare and contrast Appalachian culture with your own and draw conclusions.

Possible Assessments: Panel discussion exploring regional and cultural differences; interview representatives from both cultures and use findings in a video/radio broadcast; prepare representative works of art that highlight significant cultural differences.

Beth's unit on the Federal Government

Objective: Explain checks and balances and analyze situations where they are applicable.

Possible Assessments: Think through this scenario: "You are a political advisor to a new government in Iraq with rival Sunni, Kurdish, and Shiite factions. Advise them, based on your understanding of the U.S. Constitution and its checks and balances, how best to form a government where one element does not totally dominate the other, where decisions can be made with input from other branches and or divisions."

Susan's unit on Antarctic Emperor penguins

Objective: Determine how they survive in a hostile environment

Possible Assessments: Write a story about a pair of Emperor penguins, outlining their courtship, how they deal with rivals, cope with predators, what happens when pathways to the ocean and krill, the needed food, are temporarily blocked (by an iceberg from the Ross Ice Shelf the size of Connecticut, originally designated as B-15), and what happens when one returns and can't find its mate. Or write diary entries (patterned after Captain Scott's) of doing research on the Emperor similar to what film-makers of *March of the Penguins* might have kept.

In your judgment, which of these assessments counts as meeting Newmann's and Wiggins's criteria for being authentic? Why do you think so?

What alternatives would you have favored and why?

SELF-ASSESSMENT: INFORMAL LEARNINGS

We've mentioned several ways in which students can periodically reflect on their own progress. When we ask students to share with us what they've learned and what they find exciting and fascinating, we discover what they have made meaningful in a unit of instruction. Their questions often illuminate aspects of life we've taken for granted, for example, *"Why are school buses always yellow?"*

Here are a few such informal self-assessments:

Concept Maps: We can continue to use our Concept Maps ("What do we think we know?") throughout the unit (perhaps using different colors at different times) to record what we've been learning and answer these questions: "What surprises and fascinates me? What new questions do I have?"

Thinking/Inquiry Journals: By having students record their questions and brief summaries of their investigations, we can challenge them at various points during a unit to respond to: "What are we learning and what do I need to find out more about? What am I learning about myself as a questioner, as an investigator, as a thinker?"

These journals are excellent records of questions that students' have asked during the entire year. Depending upon students' ages, they can periodically reflect on the kinds of questions they *do* and *do not* ask and learn from their progress.

Folders/portfolios with writings: These folders might include all of the written materials created during a unit. At unit's end we can ask, "What have we learned about our own ways of thinking, ways of investigating, our own writing and analyzing of information?"

Weekly "Wraparounds": In a circle, students take turns telling "something [they] will use from information or activities learned today. Something [they] will remember from today" (Gregory & Chapman, 2002, p. 44; also, for additional ideas, see "Reflections After Learning").

Letters Home: Barbara M'Gonigle taught mathematics in Dumont, New Jersey, for many years and during that time would challenge her students to reflect on their grades and performance at key points during a marking period. "How well did you do? What were your goals and did you reach them? If not, what will you do differently in the future?" Following the reflection, Barbara

would ask her high school students to write letters home explaining their performance and presenting parents with a plan either for sustaining their excellent performance or for improving their performance. Could we use this approach, with modifications, with younger students?

One of the major benefits of challenging students in these and other ways to share what they think is important during a unit is that we learn what students have made meaningful, what has fascinated them, and what they're now curious about.

We cannot predict what students will find important, and very often we discover just how varied and amazing are the ideas they find exciting and significant.

For example, in a unit on Appalachia: "I loved the quilts and how people made them."

During the Plate Tectonics unit: "I'm fascinated by lava and different kinds of volcanoes . . . how it seeps out of earth at the Mid-Atlantic Ridge and explodes from volcanoes like St. Helens and Vesuvius."

And from a third grader reflecting on school: "Why are school buses always yellow?"

These informal learnings and questions are what fascinate us about affording students the more open opportunities to think through complex problematic situations.

CREATING ASSESSMENT RUBRICS

Of course, teachers also need evaluative criteria—criteria for students to self-assess their progress through their plans. These criteria can then be used by both teachers and students to assess the final projects.

Teachers can work with their students to develop standards to conduct an ongoing assessment of students' work. One way to proceed is to present students with a set of criteria for their final evaluation. Another is to spend class time answering the question, "What criteria or standards are we going to use to evaluate your productions?"

Teachers and students together might generate the following criteria for a project on comparative democracies, substances that endanger the environment, or heroes and heroines in literature and life:

- Manner of presentation (orally, in writing)
- Organization of material
- Creativity
- Knowledge and understanding of subject
- Reasoning process (I usually have to add this one)

Teachers can take any one of these criteria and attempt to identify the specific elements within it that would enable them to make a judgment (see Figures 8.1 and 8.2).

We can even take one of these criteria, "knowledge and understanding of subject," and further identify key elements that help us determine whether or not we really understand what we're speaking and writing about.

PRESENTATION RUBRIC

Standard: A smooth, organized presentation that exhibits understanding of the content.

Performance Criteria	1	2	3	4
Organization	No beginning, middle, or ending. Ideas not clearly stated.	Some logical structure in beginning, middle, and end but raises significant questions about logical relationships.	Logical beginning, middle, and ending with mostly strong connections among stated ideas. Raises few questions to clarify relationships.	Strong beginning, middle, and ending with logical connections among clearly stated ideas.
Creativity	Presentation follows traditional format of written or spoken report; has no novel, original elements.	Some originality in one or more elements.	Presentation includes originality in two or more elements.	Presentation represents original approaches in most areas: in use of media, of different points of view, analogies/metaphors/ models, visualizations, story elements, and redefinition of problems.
Knowledge of Content	Limited knowledge of content; inability to respond to probing questions e.g., "What if. . . ?"	Knowledge limited to presentation; difficulty responding to some follow-up questions. No performances of understanding. See 4.	Accurate information, uses one or more performances of understanding: explanations, creating relationships, use of models/ analogies. Identifying new problems and responses to "What if. . . ?" questions.	Accurate, extensive knowledge reflected in planning, presentation, and use of two or more performances of understanding: explanations, creating relationships, use of models/analogies, identifying new problems and responses to "What if. . . ?" questions and scenarios.
Reasoning	Ideas unclear, not related, and little or no logical support for conclusions.	Some ideas clear, but not related. Some supportive evidence.	Most ideas clear and related. Most conclusions logically supported.	All ideas clearly outlined and related; conclusions logically drawn from reliable, representative, evidence and unbiased sources. Can reflect on and describe reasoning processes used.

Figure 8.1

RUBRIC

Content/process:

Performance Criteria	1	2	3	4

Figure 8.2

Possible criteria for **Understanding**:

- Ability to **explain** complex issues/problems
- Facility of **relating** and **connecting** subject to similar concepts
- Ability to **apply** principles to novel situations
- Ability to create models, **metaphors,** and analogies (and explain them)
- Response to peers' questions, especially, "What if?"

I wouldn't expect students to generate these kinds of criteria, but by asking, "How do we know if you really understand these ideas and topics? What can you do to demonstrate your understandings to me?" I'll bet many students will be able to generate alternative as well as authentic assessment experiences, including some of the high levels of intellectual challenge we have identified here (Levels II and III).

Once we have the criteria, of course, it is necessary to identify what Outstanding performance might look like in all of the categories:

Explain: Explanations are extensive, including evidence that is relevant—and perhaps contrary—reliable, and representative.

Relate: Connections identify multiple significant elements that are comparable and how so; as well as characteristics not comparable and why. Draw reasonable conclusions from comparisons.

Apply: Applications are to novel situations; they fit (are appropriate) and identify logical consequences/results.

Create models/metaphors/analogies: Aspects of comparison are significant, fit appropriately, and reflect the essence of the designated referent.

Respond to peers' questions: Can respond flexibly to a variety of questions (such as, "Why? What if?") that challenge presenter to manipulate and/or rearrange elements of problem or issue in order to respond.

Developing criteria and scoring rubrics is obviously a task that teachers can perform themselves. As students become more accustomed to exercising some control over their own learning, teachers can engage them in the process so students become more responsible for the quality of their own thinking and learning.

For a wealth of assessment instruments, including rubrics, visit Kathy Schrock's Guide for Educators (2006), especially the "Rubric for a Research Project," where you will find the following criteria: Thesis/Problem/Question, Information Seeking/Evaluating, Analysis, Synthesis, Documentation, and Product/Process. What we might add to this excellent rubric is consideration for critical analysis of information (see above discussion of Lipman's and McPeck's definitions of critical thinking), searching for reliability of sources; kinds of evidence, underlying assumptions, definitions, and bias or slant.

A rubric for Critical Thinking might include any of these criteria:

- Identifies main issue or question and data related thereto
- Recognizes bias, importance of context, and point of view where appropriate
- Questions and analyzes underlying, unspoken assumptions (McPeck)
- Presents and analyzes alternative points of view, some with evidence contradictory of own conclusions
- Creates valid comparisons, metaphors, models, and analogies
- Draws own conclusions, based upon reliable, representative, unbiased evidence
- Identifies criteria/standards for making judgments and claims (Lipman)
- Outlines what we do not know, cannot yet determine

A Google search will reveal many variations on the above. One to consider is The Critical Thinking Rubric (2002).

AGAIN, SELF-ASSESSMENT

Teachers can use these criteria for student self-assessment, for student group assessments of each other's performances, as well as for their own assessment of students. One strategy teachers might consider is to have students evaluate themselves using these criteria, for teachers to do the same, and then for students and teachers to sit down together and compare perceptions and arrive at common understandings. Better yet, teachers can do this kind of negotiation of perceptions midway through the unit and just before presentation so students have a pretty clear idea of how well they are doing.

Assessment seems to be a far easier task to undertake when students and teachers are engaged in purposeful, long-term investigations of worthwhile answers to questions posed by both. That is to say, teachers do not have to fret about how to assess students' comprehension of materials that they have "covered" when students have been actively pursuing their own, the class's, and the teacher's questions.

Assessment is ongoing from the beginning of the KWHLAQ process, "This is what I/we know and do not know," to the end, "This is what we have learned." The challenging questions are, "How can students share the wealth of knowledge they have gathered from these inquiries? What forms of public reporting will most beneficially demonstrate the depth and quality of their understanding of the important ideas, concepts, and skills?"

BEYOND THE CLASSROOM DOORS

The final element in the KWHLAQ process (see Chapter 5), application and transfer to novel situations, has been stressed throughout this exploration of PBL. Not too much is written about this most important process (Fogarty, Perkins, & Barell, 1992).

Figure 8.3   Bridging Beyond the Classroom

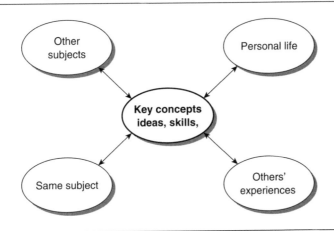

It stands to reason that teachers want students to leave classrooms with ideas and skills they can use in the real world. This is the heart of Perkins' (1992) assertion that the major goals of education are acquisition of knowledge, understanding, performance, and using or applying this knowledge in other contexts. Bloom (1956) calls this process application; he wedged it in between comprehension and analysis. It makes sense to think about transferring what students have learned after they have reflected on it and have become aware of what they have learned, not only about content, but about themselves as researchers, scientists, historians, and about how well they can collaborate with others. This applies to students as well as to teachers. Both learn from each other and both can benefit from transferring ideas, concepts, and skills beyond the classroom (see Figure 8.3).

Integrating Learning

Making connections is a fundamental part of learning new material. Teachers need to relate the new to the old, to make as many connections as possible with what they know. This, says Johnson (1975), extends the "meaningfulness" of what students are studying. For example, studying the cell in biology invites students to relate the concept of cells to politics, religion, and social and computer sciences. Each extension is an elaboration on the meaning; therefore, transfer and application questions are ways of extending the meaning of any concept or idea.

With this in mind, there are questions teachers need to begin adding to their repertoire (Fogarty, 1989) during "Integrating/Connecting Time" periods:

- Where else have I seen these ideas or concepts? in what other contexts? subjects? where in my personal life beyond school? What are the connections or the relationships?
- Where do I think I can use some of these concepts and skills?
- Can I identify a time when I might have used some of what I am learning?

- What kind of problematic situation am I confronting now? How is it similar to others I have encountered? How is it different? What strategies can I use to work through it?

Once these questions have been posed and teachers have some answers, for example, "Yesterday I could have used my awareness of the need to stop, think, and deliberate about alternatives," both students and teachers are empowered to control their own lives more fully. Application and transfer questions, like metacognition itself, are ways for students to increase their awareness and control of their own thinking and feeling.

Then there are certain generic processes that might be gleaned from all the work on PBL. If teachers and students reflect on beginning, middle, and ending processes, students discover that they are learning about a lot more than just the federal judiciary system, for example; they are also learning about relationships and survival. Students learn very significant processes, such as the following:

- Identifying the problem within social, political, or cultural situations
- Being able to analyze complex phenomena (e.g., Exactly how do we go about analyzing—breaking something down into parts? How does this really work?)
- Posing significant or powerful questions about the situations
- Searching out answers
- Working collaboratively with colleagues
- Analyzing findings and bringing data together in meaningful patterns
- Presenting new ideas
- Reflecting on proceedings, processes, and learnings

These learnings are just as important as what many call traditional content. Teachers who tap into them will undoubtedly enhance thinking, teaching, and learning processes immensely!

Stop and Think

 What intellectual and/or social processes can you identify in PBL and how or where can you use them in other settings?

THE END OF THE JOURNEY

Thus, the application and transfer process marks the end of the journey through a form of intellectual challenge that students of all abilities and diverse backgrounds deserve to encounter. Schools will never reach their potential until all students are intellectually challenged, emotionally and physically involved, and engaged at their highest levels of potential. PBL is a process that invites teachers and students to integrate complex phenomena, find answers, and apply what they have learned. The more teachers and students travel along these pathways, the richer their intellectual and emotional lives will be, especially if they are accompanied by persons with similar interests.

In the words of the old mariner, Ulysses, as he sets forth for one more thrilling experience:

Come, my friends,

'Tis not too late to seek a newer world.

Push off, and sitting well in order smite

The sounding furrows; for my purpose holds

To sail beyond the sunset, and the baths

Of all the western stars, until I die.

"Ulysses," by Alfred, Lord Tennyson

What's My Thinking Now

Reflection

Comments

Questions

Resource A

*Alternative Sample Units
for Teacher-Directed Inquiry*

The following are some alternative problems for teachers using teacher-directed inquiry to pose. Following these two high school examples are several "You are . . . " problematic situations from elementary and middle school teachers.

HIGH SCHOOL UNITS IN SCIENCE AND HISTORY

Biology[1]

Content: Study of nature, functions, and effects of bacteria on human body

Objectives: Students will . . .
- Be able to identify different kinds of bacteria found in human bodies
- Compare roles of good and bad bacteria and how they function in our bodies
- Set procedures for determining extent of bacteria in specific physical locations, analyze results, draw conclusions and share findings with students and school authorities

Problematic Situation

You are a member of a research team invited into a school to respond to complaints that living and eating conditions in the building are unsanitary. You are charged with investigating the extent of bacteria in places in the building you think are important and making a report to the Board of Education with your findings and recommendations.

Strategy Possibilities

1. Discuss the problem with the whole class. Engage them in analyzing the situation: "What do we know? What do we need to know?" Encourage

them to ask as many questions as possible to understand the situation. Form small investigative groups and instruct them to make initial hypotheses: "Where would you expect to find most bacteria and why?" Post hypotheses by group and record reasoning.

2. In their small research groups, have students plan out a strategy: How will they gather information, protect validity of findings (against contamination), and so on. (Core experience)

3. Have each group investigate and analyze its findings, draw conclusions, and make recommendations to the whole class. Students should be prepared to answer probing "Why?" and "What if?" questions to assess understanding.

4. Help groups compare their initial hypotheses with their final results and determine reasons for any discrepancies before and after. (Culminating experience)

5. Ask, "What have we learned about bacteria? about ourselves as investigative scientists? What are our research questions now? How can we apply what we have learned to further investigations? to our next units of study? to other areas of our school and personal lives" (e.g., about making quick guesses, jumping to conclusions, relying on assumptions, etc.)?

Evaluation Possibilities

1. Use final reports as assessments with criteria developed by the teacher and published beforehand.

2. Each group makes presentation of findings to class and responds to "Why?" "What if?" and other probing questions. Teams self-assess using rubric created by the entire class. Each team will find creative ways to share findings (e.g., using interviews, video, computer graphics, PowerPoint, etc.)

3. Have each student write a concluding summary of the investigation and personal recommendations. Have each include responses to questions: "What did I learn? How can I apply findings within biology, within other subjects, and in my personal life?"

High School History[2]

Problematic Situation

The year is 1763 and you have just been named British Minister of the Treasury. Your job is to devise a plan to help Britain reduce the debt of 147 million pounds. The debt has doubled over the past seven years, due to the French and Indian Wars, which Britain financed for the colonies. You should be aware that the average British citizen is paying twenty-six times the taxes of the average American colonist. The colonies cost the British in administrative fees four times the amount that Britain collects from the colonies in taxes. The last time taxes were raised in Britain, there was a violent tax revolt. What will you do? Carefully discuss the matter with your advisors, make your decision and then prepare to present it to Parliament and the King.

"YOU ARE . . . ." PROBLEMATIC SITUATIONS DEVELOPED BY ELEMENTARY AND MIDDLE SCHOOL TEACHERS

Kindergarten/Grade 1: "You are a meteorologist looking for a job. NBC wants to hire you but they need proof that you know and understand the water cycle. They need to see written records of your observations. They also need predictions on experiments and results of them, too. Finally, you will receive a $1000 salary raise if you can draw a diagram of the water cycle and label it." (for students with special needs)

Grades 2/3: "You are a member of the principal's advisory committee on redesigning the school playground. Examine what we have now: what kinds of play equipment exist on the playground currently. Determine what you think we need. How will you gather information and from whom? Then plan out what would be an ideal playground. Make sketches of your plan. Figure out how you would present this plan to the principal and parents. Be prepared to tell why you think each piece of equipment belongs on a playground." (Ann Marie Pantano and Brian Mackoul, Upper Montclair, NJ)

Grade 3/4: "You are a member of a research team investigating the changes in the Great Barrier Reef in Queensland, Australia. The Reef is slowly dying in places. You need to determine why so many corals are not growing, the extent of the damage, and projected consequences. You need to analyze this situation and determine what can be done about this unfortunate phenomenon. Upon arriving at reasonable conclusions you will share your findings and recommendations with local authorities."

Middle School: "You are a committee of residents of a small town in an upper Midwestern state. A recent geological survey team has found coal and oil deposits in a nearby mountain range about 50 miles distant. The American Energy Company is planning a presentation before the mayor, town council, and concerned citizens during which it hopes to receive public approval to proceed with local mining and/or drilling. The mayor has asked you and committee members (all residents representing families, local businesses, hospitals, energy companies, and schools) to prepare background research on mining procedures and ecological impact and to identify key questions that need to be asked and appropriately answered before operations can be approved. Your report will be presented to the mayor and to AEC."

Middle School/High School: "You are a member of a town planning committee responsible for preparing a welcome and smooth integration of a rather large group of immigrants from across the border/overseas. You need to investigate their own culture and how to ensure smooth transitions in terms of education, business, access to all public services, and opportunities to share their own cultural heritage. You will make your recommendations to public officials and local leaders."

Middle/High School: "You have recently been called into the town of Ording, Washington, which lies at the base of Mt. Rainier. It is predicted that a pyroclastic flow will occur sometime in the near future. Such a natural disaster jeopardizes the lives of almost 200,000 people. Develop and build a protective device to offset the power of the phenomenon, thereby saving the lives and protecting the property of the Ording population." (Anna Arrigo, teacher, Newark, NJ)

NOTES

1. This unit was developed by Vin Frick from Dumont High School, Dumont, New Jersey.

2. This unit was developed by Paul Amoroso from Pompton Lakes High School, Pompton Lakes, New Jersey.

References

Baird, J., & White, R. (1984, April). *Improving learning through enhanced metacognition: A classroom study.* Paper presented at the annual meeting of the American Educational Research Association, New Orleans.

Bandura, A. (1986). *Social foundations of thought and action: A cognitive theory.* Englewood Cliffs, NJ: Prentice Hall.

Barell, J. (1980). *Playgrounds of our minds.* New York: Teachers College Press.

Barell, J. (1992). *. . . Ever wonder . . . ?* Columbus, OH: Zaner-Bloser.

Barell, J. (1995). *Teaching for thoughtfulness* (2nd ed.). White Plains, NY: Longman.

Barell, J. (2003). *Developing more curious minds.* Alexandria, VA: Association for Supervision and Curriculum Development.

Bloom, B. (1956). *Taxonomy of educational objectives: Cognitive domain.* New York: David McKay.

Bransford, J., Brown, A., & Cocking, R. R. (Eds.). (2000). *How people learn—Brain, mind, experience, and school.* Washington, DC: National Academy Press.

Bransford, J., Franks, J., Vye, N., & Sherwood, R. (1986, June). *New approaches to instruction: Because wisdom can't be taught.* Paper presented at a conference on Similarity and Analogy at the University of Illinois, Champaign-Urbana.

Bronowski, J. (1965). *Science and human values.* New York: Harper Perennial Library.

Bronowski, J. (1978). *The origins of knowledge and imagination.* New Haven, CT: Yale University Press.

Byrd, R. E. (1938). *Alone.* New York: Putnam's.

Byrd, R. E. (1956, August). All-out assault on Antarctica. *National Geographic Magazine, 110*(2), 141–180.

Caine, R., & Caine, G. (1997). *Education on the edge of possibility.* Alexandria, VA: Association for Supervision and Curriculum Development.

Career education and consumer, family, and life skills. 2005. In *New Jersey Core Curriculum Content Standards.* Accessed August 2006 from the New Jersey Department of Education Web site: http://www.state.nj.us/njded/cccs/s9_career .htm#92

Cisneros, C. (1989). *The house on Mango Street.* New York: Vintage Contemporaries.

Cooper, L. (Trans.). (1977). *Plato: On the trial and death of Socrates.* London: Cornell University Press.

The Critical Thinking Rubric. (2002). Retrieved May 2006 from http://wsuctproject .wsu.edu/ctr.htm

Dalziel, I. W. D. (1995). Earth before Pangaea. *Scientific American, 272*(1), 58–63.

Dewey, J. (1933). *How we think.* Lexington, MA: D. C. Heath.

Dewey, J. (1963). *Democracy and education.* New York: Macmillan.

Dillon, J. T. (1984). Research on questioning and discussion. *Educational Leadership, 42*(3, November), 50–56.

Dillon, J. T. (1988). *Questioning and teaching: A manual of practice.* New York: Teachers College Press.

Elmore, F., Peterson, P., & McCarthey, S. (1996). *Restructuring in the classroom: Teaching, learning, and school organization.* San Francisco: Jossey-Bass.

Fogarty, R. (1989). *From training to transfer: The role of creativity in the adult learner.* Unpublished doctoral dissertation, Loyola University, Chicago.

Fogarty, R. (1991). *The mindful school: How to integrate the curricula.* Palatine, IL: Skylight.

Fogarty, R. (1994). *The mindful school: How to teach for metacognitive reflection.* Arlington Heights, IL: IRI/SkyLight.

Fogarty, R. (1997). *Problem-based learning & other curriculum models for the multiple intelligences classroom.* Thousand Oaks, CA: Corwin Press.

Fogarty, R., Perkins, D., & Barell, J. (1992). *The mindful school: How to teach for transfer.* Palatine, IL: Skylight.

Fullan, M. (1993). *Change forces in education: Probing the depths of educational reform.* London: Falmer.

Fullan, M. (2001). *Leading in a culture of change.* San Francisco: Jossey-Bass.

Goodlad, J. (1984). *A place called school.* New York: McGraw-Hill.

Gregory, G., & Chapman, C. (2002). *Differentiated instructional strategies—One size doesn't fit all.* Thousand Oaks, CA: Corwin Press.

Hmelo, C. (1994). *The cognitive effects of problem based learning: A preliminary study.* (ERIC Document Reproduction Service No. ED 371026)

In search of human origins. (1997). Transcript available at http://www.pbs.org/wgbh/nova/transcripts/2106hum1.html

Introduction. (n.d.). Retrieved May 2006 from the New Jersey Core Curriculum Standards Web site at http://www.state.nj.us/njded/cccs/intro.htm

Johnson, R. (1975). Meaning in complex learning. *Review of Educational Research, 45,* 425–460.

Kathy Schrock's guide for educators. (2006). Retrieved July 24, 2006, from http://school.discovery.com/schrockguide/assess.html

Lipman, M. (1988). Critical thinking: What it can be. *Cogitare, 2*(4), 1–2.

Lipman, M., Sharp, A., & Oscanyan, F. (1980). *Philosophy in the classroom.* Philadelphia: Temple University Press.

Louis, K., & Miles, M. (1990). *Improving the urban high school: What works and why.* New York: Teachers College Press.

McCarthy, B. (1987). *The 4 MAT system: Teaching to learning styles with right/left mode techniques.* Barrington, IL: EXCEL.

McCombs, B. (1991, April). *Metacognition and motivation for higher level thinking.* Paper presented at the annual meeting of the American Educational Research Association, Chicago.

Manteno Community Unit School District #5. (2006). Retrieved August 2006 from http://www.manteno5.org/webquest

Marzano, R. (2003). *What works in schools—Translating research into action.* Alexandria, VA: Association for Supervision and Curriculum Development.

Marzano, R., Pickering. D., & McTighe, J. (1992). *A different kind of classroom: Teaching with dimensions of thinking.* Alexandria, VA: Association for Supervision and Curriculum Development.

Marzano, R., Pickering, D. J., & Pollock, J. E. (2001). *Classroom instruction that works—Research based strategies for increasing student achievement.* Alexandria, VA: Association for Supervision and Curriculum Development.

Marzano R., Waters, T., & McNulty, B. (2005). *School leadership that works—From research to results.* Alexandria, VA: Association for Supervision and Curriculum Development.

Mayer, R. (1989). Models for understanding. *Review of Educational Research, 59,* 43–64.

McPeck, J. (1981). *Critical thinking and education.* Oxford, UK: Martin Robertson.

Mid-continent Education and Learning (McREL). (n.d.). Available online at http://mcrel.org

National Education Association. (2006). Available online at http://www.nea.org/classroom/curr-standards.html

Newmann, F., & associates. (1996). *Authentic achievement: Restructuring schools for intellectual quality.* San Francisco: Jossey-Bass.

Norell, M. (2001). The proof is in the plumage. *Natural History, 110*(6), 58–63.

Norman, G. (1992). *Reports findings on effectiveness of problem based learning in medical school education.* (ERIC Document Reproduction Service No. EJ 451745)

Olge, D. (1986). K-W-L: A teaching model that develops active reading of expository text. *Reading Teacher, 39,* 564–571.

O'Shea, M. R. (2005). *From standards to success.* Alexandria, VA: Association for Supervision and Curriculum Development.

Parker, J. (1970). *Process as content.* New York: Rand McNally.

Paulsen, G. (1987). *Hatchet.* New York: Penguin/Puffin.

Perkins, D. (1992). *Smart schools.* New York: Basic Books.

Pizzolato, P. (1996). *Fables: Storytelling in the foreign language classroom.* Upper Montclair, NJ: Montclair State University Press.

Plate tectonics and climate change. (n.d.). Retrieved July 19, 2006, from http://earth.usc.edu/~stott/Catalina/platetectonics.html

Pressley, M. (1987, April). *What is good strategy use and why is it hard to teach?: An optimistic appraisal of the challenges associated with strategy instruction.* Paper presented at the annual meeting of the American Educational Research Association, Washington, D.C.

Rowe, F., & Webb, W. (Eds.). (1938). *Tennyson.* London: Macmillan.

SCANS. (1991). *What work requires of schools: A SCANS report for America 2000* [Executive Summary]. Washington, DC: U.S. Department of Labor, Secretary's Commission on Achieving Necessary Skills.

Sigel, I., Copple, C., & Saunders, R. (1984). *Educating the young thinker.* Hillsdale, NJ: Lawrence Erlbaum.

Sizer, T. (1992). *Horace's school: Redesigning the American high school.* Boston: Houghton Mifflin.

Social studies. (2006). Retrieved September 2006 from the New Jersey Core Curriculum Web Site at http://www.state.nj.us/njded/cccs/s6_ss.htm

Sounds of Antarctica. (2005). Retrieved July 24, 2006, from the Web site of the Australian Antarctic Division at http://www.aad.gov.au/default.asp?casid=229

Stepien, W., Gallagher, S., & Workman, D. (1992). *Problem-based learning for traditional and interdisciplinary classrooms.* Aurora: Illinois Mathematics and Science Academy, Center for Problem-Based Learning.

Sternberg, R. (1985). *Beyond IQ: A triarchic theory of human intelligence.* New York: Oxford University Press.

Stevens, H., & Stigler, J. (1992). *The learning gap.* New York: Simon & Schuster.

Swartz, R., & Perkins, D. (1989). *Teaching thinking: Issues and approaches.* Pacific Grove, CA: Midwest.

Tomlinson, C. A. (1999). *The differentiated classroom—Responding to the needs of all learners.* Alexandria, VA: Association for Supervision and Curriculum Development.

Tyler, R. (1949). *Basic principles of curriculum and instruction.* Chicago: University of Chicago Press.

Walker, A. (1982). *The color purple.* New York: Simon & Schuster.

Welch, J., with J. A. Byrne. (2001). *Jack: Straight from the gut.* New York: Warner Business Books.

Wiggins, G. (1993). *Assessing student performance: Exploring the purpose and limits of testing.* San Francisco: Jossey-Bass.

Wiggins, G. (1998). *Educative assessment: Designing assessments to inform and improve student performance.* San Francisco: Jossey-Bass.

Index

CORWIN PRESS

The Corwin Press logo—a raven striding across an open book—represents the union of courage and learning. Corwin Press is committed to improving education for all learners by publishing books and other professional development resources for those serving the field of PreK–12 education. By providing practical, hands-on materials, Corwin Press continues to carry out the promise of its motto: **"Helping Educators Do Their Work Better."**